Machine Learning For Beginners

Complete AI for Beginners with Real-world Business Applications

Declan Mellor

ISBN: 9798633569544

Table of Contents

MACHINE LEARNING FOR BEGINNERS   ERROR! BOOKMARK NOT DEFINED.

INTRODUCTION   5

INTRODUCTION   5

THE PURPOSE OF THIS BOOK   7

WHAT IS ARTIFICIAL INTELLIGENCE?   11

HOW IS MACHINE LEARNING USED?   18

RECENT IMPROVEMENTS IN DATA ANALYSIS   23

IMAGE RECOGNITION   25

VOICE RECOGNITION   28

MEDICINE AND MEDICAL DIAGNOSIS   29

STOCK FORECASTS   30

LEARNING ASSOCIATIONS   32

FINANCE   35

SPAM DETECTION   36

INTRODUCTION TO STATISTICS   38

CHOOSING THE RIGHT TYPE OF MODEL FOR MACHINE LEARNING   44

LEARNING UNDER SUPERVISION   47

REGRESSION ANALYSIS   48

DECISION TREES   59

RANDOM FORESTS   61

CLASSIFICATIONS   63

LOGISTIC REGRESSION / CLASSIFICATION   65

K NEAREST NEIGHBORS   66

VECTOR SUPPORT   68

KERNEL SUPPORT VECTOR   68

NAIVE BAYES   70

LEARNING WITHOUT SUPERVISION   70

CLUSTERING   73

K-MEANS CLUSTERING   73

DIMENSIONALITY REDUCTION   74

NEURAL NETWORKS   75

LEARNING REINFORCEMENT   82
Q LEARNING   83
SEMI-GUIDED LEARNING   84
ENSEMBLE MODELLING   84
THINGS YOU NEED TO KNOW FOR MACHINE LEARNING   87
DATA   87
PREPARE THE DATA   90
PROGRAMMING TOOLS   92
DEVELOP MODELS   95
ANACONDA FOR PYTHON   96
ALGORITHMS   98
VISUALIZATION TOOLS   98
MORE ADVANCED THINGS THAT ARE USEFUL   99
EPILOGUE   101

Introduction

Congratulations on purchasing Machine Learning for beginners and thank you for doing so.

There are many possibilities in the field of machine learning. It is used as a tool by almost every major industry. Whether you are interested in healthcare, business and finance, agriculture, clean energy and many others, there is someone who uses the power of machine learning to make their job easier. Unfortunately for these industries, but luckily for you, there is a huge shortage of talent in the field of data science and artificial intelligence. While entry-level data science jobs remain competitive, there is a significant shortage of experienced data professionals who can perform the high-level functions. It is a newer field in computer science, with a younger group of individuals making up for much of the field.

It can be very financially rewarding if you manage to get a job in data science. In 2016, the average data scientist made about $ 111,000, with predicted growth over the next five years. About half of the data scientists working in the field have a Ph.D. It is not a requirement, but it is something to think about if you are looking for a real career as a data scientist.

If you want to add machine learning to your wheelhouse so that you can better understand and implement it in your own company or projects, a Ph.D. may not be necessary. But for those looking to enter the field, higher education is recommended as it will help you stand out from the field.

Indeed.com called machine learning the best career in 2019 and it's easy to see why. With a huge demand for talented data scientists and a lucrative payoff, it's worth checking out. And big data doesn't seem to be disappearing anytime soon with increasing connectivity and internet use by consumers and businesses more than ever. Data is part of our modern world, and as the complexity and size of data increases, even more specialized knowledge and skills will be required to complete the task.

To supplement the knowledge in this book, I strongly recommend seeking more knowledge in statistics and programming. A good foundation of statistical knowledge is required to perform any work in machine learning, because statistical mathematics provides the structure and justification for all models and algorithms that data scientists use for machine learning.

The purpose of this book

This book is not intended to be a comprehensive machine learning textbook. Instead, it gives you a foundation of knowledge to continue your studies of machine learning and artificial intelligence. To continue your studies and master the subject, a great deal of study has to be done. Discusses the general structure and organization of machine learning models, the general terms and basic statistical concepts necessary to use and understand machine learning.
To be a data scientist requires an understanding of statistics and quantitative analysis. After all, artificial intelligence and machine learning are rooted in statistics. This provides the anchor and foundation for the type of math required.
While coding is not required to understand this book, it is an important part of machine learning. In order to process large amounts of data, data scientists must have working knowledge of computer programming to "tell" the data what they want them to do. This book doesn't provide much information about coding, but it will provide resources and ways to get you started on coding your own. In any case, by the end of the book I will help you set up Python with the necessary libraries and toolkits to help you learn how to program.

The most used language in machine learning is Python. It is a versatile language that is relatively easy to learn and freely available. Python packages are designed for data analysis to speed up your encoding. C ++ is also fairly common, but more difficult to master. A third option is R, which is quite popular because it is free and open source. Students often use it for its availability and simplicity. The downside to using R is that it can't handle huge data sets commonly used in machine learning and artificial intelligence, which is somewhat limiting.

Machine learning computers are distinguished for not only remembering new information, but applying it to new situations in the future. There is a difference between remembering and learning. There is an important distinction between giving a code line to a computer and creating a machine learning model.

The basic feature of machine learning is the use of artificial inductive reasoning. Artificial inductive reasoning means that a specific event gives you reason to generalize a characteristic. This apple is green; therefore, all apples must be green. But here you can see why inductive reasoning in itself is not always perfect and why it is difficult to train computers to follow the same thought process. A given piece of data is not necessarily representative of thousands of other possible pieces of data. Therefore, when we use statistics and machine learning, we need to use enough data to reason with confidence, without drawing the wrong conclusion from data that is misinterpreted and misleading.

There are things we do every day as human beings that we consider "common sense." These kinds of intuitive decisions cannot be explicitly programmed into a computer, because the variables that help us make our decisions are too difficult to measure. We probably don't need to see a thousand different combinations of chess pieces on a chessboard to think and plan ahead when we get into a situation we haven't seen before. We as humans need much less data to be able to derive and learn.

This is where machine learning comes into play. In these situations where the variables are complex and directions cannot be explicitly stated, they need to be learned. Back to the example of a computer that can play checkers. It would take far too long to teach someone to play checkers by giving them all possible moves and all possible countermoves. Instead, you teach someone the basics, and through play, the person learns what helps them win and what doesn't.

Likewise, it is impossible to tell your computer all possible situations in a drafts game and then tell the computer what to do in each situation. There are far too many options. Instead, you should provide the computer with enough data so that it can respond accordingly even when faced with a new situation.

Another example we'll talk about later in this book uses artificial neural networks to sort whether a photo is an image of a cat or a dog. As a human, this type of classification would be too easy. We know what a dog looks like because we've seen dogs, and we know what a cat looks like because we've seen cats.

But there is no way to explicitly tell a computer how to tell the difference between a cat and a dog. Instead, give the computer a set of training data with pictures of cats and dogs, and tell the computer which pictures are cats and which pictures are dogs. Ultimately, the model should be able to tell you if new, unseen photos include a feline or a canine tooth.

The problem with explicitly programmed instructions is their inability to change. If I tell a computer exactly what to do, using a programming language with explicit instructions, the program will do that job very well, but only that job. It doesn't change when it gets new information and it doesn't change the method if it doesn't work properly

Over time, a machine learning model will be able to change itself as the data changes so that it continues to adapt and remain accurate in a changing unaccompanied environment. This offers a huge advantage because it makes our models more adaptable to changes that are constantly around us. Without machine learning and artificial intelligence, our computers would have no way to keep up.

What is artificial intelligence?

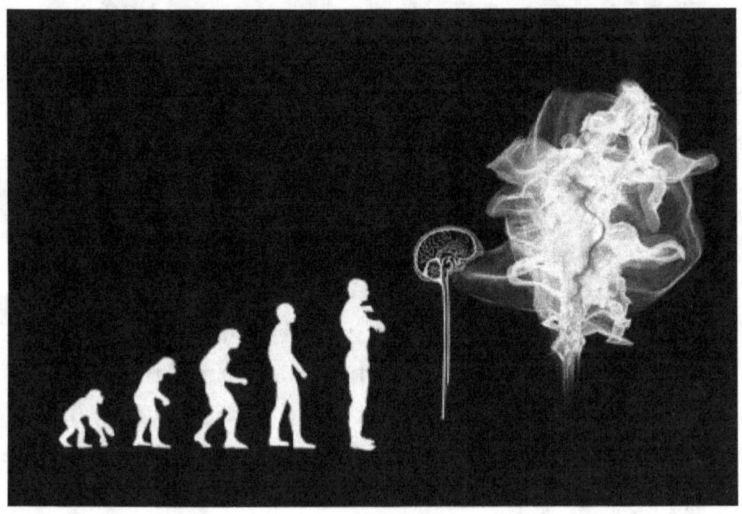

In the 1950s, individual researchers started developing the first machines for artificial intelligence. Previously, only small experiments had been conducted with artificial intelligence; especially when cracking codes during World War II. It was an emerging field and only a few people seemed to be aware of the potential at first

Now artificial intelligence is used in a variety of applications across multiple sectors, including problem solving, learning, planning, reasoning and logic. It enables computers to perform tasks that normally require human thinking. To 'think' like a person, computers need data from which they can learn.

Artificial intelligence has an almost mythical place in people's minds. I bet if you said the words artificial intelligence to most people, there would be images of robots walking around like humans. This kind of science fictionalization of artificial intelligence makes people wary when they hear the term. But it is not as scary as it sounds. It has done a lot of good in medicine and business, transportation and communication. While impressive progress has been made in the field, the delusion of a conscious computer is still a long way off. Yet the emergence of self-driving cars and computers and telephones that can talk stirs the imagination.

While it sounds more like something from science fiction, artificial intelligence is now in so much of our daily lives. If it sounded spooky to you at first, let me remind you of all the technology that artificial intelligence has brought to our lives in recent years.

The last time you turned on Netflix, you browsed through a list of the shows you watched and the movies you watched again. It turned that list into data and created another list of recommendations. It predicted movies you would enjoy based on what you already liked. This is done through machine learning, a subset of artificial intelligence.

If you have a smartphone, you can use voice commands to search for things hands-free. You tell your phone that you are looking for cafes in your area and your phone says "Search cafes in your area." Within a few seconds, a list of results will appear and you don't even have to type anything. It recognized your voice and understood what you were saying. This is part of natural language processing, another subset of machine learning. Every time you open your email account and you tag spam; your email host will learn how to better identify spam. This is another type of machine learning.

Artificial intelligence is therefore not necessarily conscious robots that want to take over as we know it. From now on, it is much more favorable than that. It is also extremely useful and it can teach things for which we cannot explicitly program it. Artificial intelligence requires something called artificial reasoning, also known as machine reasoning. When people learn new things and draw conclusions, we go through a process known as inductive reasoning. We take pieces of information to draw new conclusions. Usually there is no hard and fast rule to teach. We learn from experience and draw our own rules through cumulative experience. For example, I could tell you

that it snowed 15 times last December. Therefore, it will snow again this December. Every day in January was cold, so every day in January will be cold. So I have to bring a jacket.

We weren't born wired to know that snow would fall in December, or that January would be cold. We learned these things through experience and used inductive reasoning to generalize about future December and January periods. Based on our inductive reasoning, we make the logical decision to prepare and bring a jacket next winter.

The experiences we had with snow in December and cold in January represent our "data". These are the input of our environment from which we constantly learn.

People think differently than machines because we don't interpret numerical data patterns. We learn from positive and negative rewards and from the feelings we experience in our daily lives. By having a computer use inductive reasoning, we get closer to "human-like" machines

So to learn computers, they need data to learn from. Data usually needs to be numeric so that it can be interpreted by mathematical models and algorithms. If we give a computer enough data, it will create the parameters to design its own model or algorithm, to predict new situations based on previous experience. This is the basis of machine learning. Power the computing experience so that it can predict new results in the future through inductive reasoning.

Artificial intelligence is particularly interesting because computers are already better than humans for some tasks. They can draw mathematical conclusions about a dataset with thousands of inputs in seconds. No human on earth could process that kind of information so quickly. If we could use machine learning to examine data from a complex data set of 100 variables, we could probably learn more about trends and patterns that were very complex and difficult to distinguish manually. This is what makes computers such a useful tool and why they have contributed to massive advances in data science. Using computers for data analysis makes it easier to find patterns and matches that you don't even know exist or that may not even have been considered.

Computers perform very poorly in other tasks. Some of these tasks seem very simple to us. Like identifying the difference between a photo of a cat and a photo of a dog. But for a computer, this is extremely complicated to figure out. Therein lies the current challenge with artificial intelligence. Bridging that gap between the type of inductive reasoning that people can do and the type of reasoning computers is good at that.

Key concept: inductive reasoning. Using information from experiences and our environment to draw generalizations. The ability to tell the difference between these photos based on our knowledge of cats and dogs; this is what we know as reasoning. The goal of artificial intelligence is to teach computers how to have the same skills as human reasoning

Computer models have been used to process natural languages. Natural language processing gives computers the ability to understand "natural" languages, or what we know as our human languages. Natural language processing is based on machine learning techniques to understand speech and text and to respond to commands and interactions.

This technology is becoming very common and accessible. GPUs (graphics processing units) are becoming more widely available and cheaper, which means that data sets are getting bigger and the use of machine learning is increasing. You may have used it when talking to Siri on your iPhone. When you say something to Siri, your phone will receive the audio. To interpret it, it turns your audio into text. Your phone then analyzes the text to derive meaning from the command you gave it.

Natural language processing is one of the most common uses of machine learning and we use it every day. When we use a web search function, we use natural language processing. Translation apps need to take our voice or our text and analyze the sentence structure to gain meaning. When you type a paper or word document, your word processor uses natural language processing to look for grammatical and spelling mistakes.

Despite its popularity, it is a very complex field of computer science and artificial intelligence. Being able to interpret the meaning of the alphabet in an almost infinite amount of combinations requires vast amounts of data for the computer to understand what you are writing or saying.

Besides being able to understand what we say and write; computers can also make strategic decisions based on what they learned from data in the 1990s. IBM created a computer called Deep Blue that defeated a world chess master. It was the first computer to perform such a task. Because of the simplicity of the rules in chess, computer scientists at IBM chose to train their computers to play. But there are thousands of possible moves and arrangements that the pieces can take on once the game has started. The computer had to learn this using data.

What makes machine learning unique for other forms of computer science is the ability of models to change their methods over time to adapt new data. What distinguishes a machine learning model from a regular line with explicit code is that machine learning absorbs new data and improves itself. It can also perform tasks that require planning and contain strategic components. The Deep Blue computer had to be adept at analyzing possible strings of motion, rather than just one motion at a time.

The same technologies that allowed a computer to beat a world chess champion now allow self-driving vehicles to get a passenger safely from point A to point B. Compared to the relative simplicity of chess, self-driving cars must plan and interpret hundreds of variables to keep the passenger safe. It goes beyond the two-dimensional data analysis used by chess machines. Self-driving cars must master multi-dimensional data analysis to navigate the ever-changing environment on the road.

The machine learns through trial and error, repeats the task over and over, and learns from failures and successes. These experiences are introduced as data and over time the machine will know the probability of failure or success with every possible movement.

Machine learning models interpret potential conditions in the environment. For an algorithm that plays chess, these are all possible moves and all possible moves by the competitor. The algorithm is an amalgamation of goals and possible actions. By using this data, a plan is drawn up to optimize the chances of achieving the goals. It also allows computers to self-learn without specific prompts through programming.

Trying to get a computer to do all these things sounds simpler in theory than in practice. Most of the features we just mentioned; from dams to self-driving cars require advanced statistical techniques to optimize the outcome and train a machine that knows how to 'win' with a high degree of accuracy.

Machine learning falls under the larger umbrella of artificial intelligence. Artificial intelligence is a branch of computer science that includes reasoning, natural language processing, planning and machine learning. The term was first coined by a computer scientist named John McCarthy in 1956. You will also hear the term data science, which includes artificial intelligence and machine learning. Data science is a broader term, but is often used to describe machine learning. Machine learning experts are often referred to as data scientists, both in this book and beyond. There is an overlap between data science and machine learning, but it is not the same. Data science is more of a general term, while machine learning is part of data science.

How is machine learning used?

Machine learning is a popular buzzword today. You have often thrown around the term machine learning, especially in data science for digital marketing. Other familiar terms such as artificial intelligence, data science and data mining may seem synonymous with machine learning. There are minor differences between these different fields, all of which fall under the umbrella of data science.
Data science is the management and analysis of data, and within data science there are many ways to analyze the data and use it to learn. Machine learning is his own field within computer science. The idea is to predict something and, as you add more data, compare predictions to actual outputs. Over time, your forecasting ability should improve and errors will decrease.
One of the most important functions of the human brain is the ability to change our behavior based on the results of past events and situations. If a situation has a positive outcome, we remember that, and in turn, if a situation has a negative outcome, we also store it in our memory. Later we will use this "data" to make decisions about new ones
situations. Over time, we learn to interpret situations, even if they are completely new, and we are not quite sure how to behave or react.

Machine learning helps us create a mathematical way to copy human learning ability over time and through a new experience. Machine learning models learn over time and improve their prediction methods, improving the outcome. Past data is collected and over time the model can make better and more accurate predictions. Over time, the program will be able to make more accurate predictions because of the new data it has received. It learns over time how it can be done better at completing a certain task.

Part of it has inspired science fiction and fueled fears that artificial intelligence will surpass us and take over the world. Ultimately, our machines will be able to do everything we can, only better. Our computers will surpass and leave us. Despite general fears, artificial intelligence is still a relatively young field with a long way to go. While it may not take over the world anytime soon, machine learning has changed the job market today and will continue to change it on its own in the future.

Jobs that used to require human thinking can now be done with machine learning. Factories, medical diagnosis and even taxis can be run with artificial intelligence and machine learning. Data is becoming an increasingly important field. Patterns in data cannot be interpreted with a human brain, so we use machines to detect patterns.

Machine learning is used in the financial sector to detect fraud. Algorithms can now detect when a financial transaction has fraud characteristics. Businesses can spot fake reviews by recognizing word patterns and timing for previously fake posts.

Our phones use speech recognition to understand what we are saying and respond to our requests. Social media use complex data analysis to recognize patterns in our photos and to see who is in a photo before we start tagging. All this is done by data collection and interpretation through machine learning. The patterns in photos that tell who appears are data that is analyzed and improved by machine learning models.

In 1959 Arthur Samuel first popularized the term 'machine learning'. As a graduate of MIT, he chose to create a computer program that could play checkers. He chose checkers because of the relative simplicity, but also because checkers contain many possible strategies. This predated IBM's deep blue, but the theory was the same. Over time, let the computer learn with new data.

The computer looked at the positions of each chess piece and every possible movement. Each move had a score with the chance of winning. The algorithm included factors such as the number of pieces on the board and the number of pieces that were cononed.

The algorithm has memorized any combination of positions it has experienced in a process called distance learning. For each of these combinations, it remembered the score of the chance of winning. In a few years, Samuel played numerous games with the machine to teach him how to play.

Machine learning was created to express what the machine did to learn how to beat opponents. The machine had to learn to play checkers and learn how to reduce its mistakes to win. It was the first time that machine learning was discussed as its own independent field of study outside of computer science or artificial intelligence.

Sandford University calls machine learning "the science of making computers act without being explicitly programmed." Samuel's computer did not need to be programmed to remember every possible move made by a king. Instead, the "experience" the machine gained served as data, learning from each game to optimize its winning strategy. Statistics provide the structure and mechanics for machine learning. Despite the birth of the term machine learning in 1959, it has only been recognized as a separate field in computer science since the 1990s with the advent of Deep Blue.

Normal computer programming uses an input command to control the model. An example of this is connecting 4 + 4 to your python window. It gives you the answer, 8. Instead machine learning uses the so-called input data. Input data is what the machine needs to learn, while input command would mean the machine is not self-learning. The programmer does not specify what he wants the answer to be. Instead, the machine interprets the data itself, making it self-learning. In machine learning, the machine takes data over time and uses it to create a new model for something.

The machine detects patterns and structure within data based entirely on statistical logic. It is entirely based on mathematical algorithms. Instead of using intuition to search for patterns, patterns are found on a quantitative and logical level by the machine learning model. The more relevant the data to which a machine is exposed, the better it understands and can predict the outcome of the model.

Machine learning is only useful if you can improve the efficiency of the task you're trying to accomplish. Before starting your data, think specifically about what you are trying to learn. What is the question you are trying to answer with your machine learning model?

The environment is always changing, and if you want to create models that are up-to-date and work in the changing environment, you need to keep learning your model with new data. If you want your data to be useful to you, you need to find a way to keep your data up to date with current questions.

Learn as much as possible about your market or the environment in which you operate. What things are you trying to understand? If you use machine learning to improve your business, find out what types of variables are your customers' choices. These are the things you want to identify and study in your models. You need to understand your topic well before you can use machine learning to study it. It is impossible to predict the future, even with machine learning at your disposal. But if you can adapt your models to the ever-changing data, you have a better chance in the long run than if you stagnate.

Before you begin, you must have sufficient knowledge of the data you choose. Where does it come from and how was it collected? In what format is it and what are the challenges in interpreting it? These are the types of questions you should be asking when you start, and I hope this book lets you take a critical look at the data before you start.

It is not a comprehensive approach to predicting the future, and it will not give you the magic formula to anticipate future business trends or stock prices. But it is an incredibly useful tool that, when used properly, can make decision making much easier.

The possibilities to experiment with machine learning are growing. Finding the right people to fill the jobs needed to develop machine learning and artificial intelligence is a challenge today. It is a specialized field and there is a shortage of people with statistical and IT knowledge to help move the field forward. This means that there is an opportunity for people who have the skills needed for machine learning.

Recent improvements in data analysis

Machine learning has changed dramatically since its beginnings in 1959, when Arthur Samuel's checkers played computer. But it has changed more in the past two decades than in its entire history, especially with the improvement of computing power. In the past, machine learning and big data analysis were very limited. Only larger companies with expensive technology could use data to make business decisions.

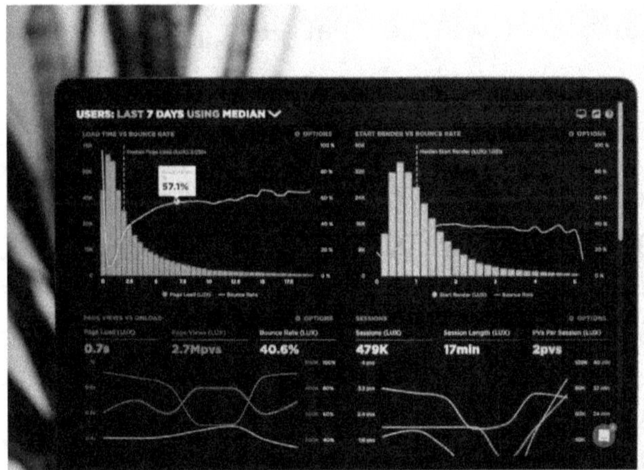

Now almost anyone can use a certain amount of data for business or other purposes with a laptop or home computer. Data is much easier to find and the machines for processing it have also become much more accessible. What used to cost expensive computing power can now be done much cheaper and faster.

The advent of cloud technology has made it easier for smaller companies to access large data sets without the need for huge amounts of data storage. Now machine learning has become a completely different field of computer science, with people specializing in machine learning and data science as their own field.

Nowadays more and more things are connected and the internet is getting bigger. This means that access to data is increasing, but data sources are also changing. Even people's cars have computers inside them, which means they create data that can be interpreted while driving. The vast majority of Americans own a mobile phone and shop the web and use apps for navigation. People use their phones to control household appliances, which is another potential data source. There are Fitbits and smartwatches that allow people to track health data.

The more devices, not just computers and telephones, but all kinds of devices connected, the greater the possibilities for collecting and studying data. This connection of everything; smartphones, smart cars, etc. make people nervous that they risk losing their private data. They fear that their privacy is at stake and that someone will always look at them. But machine learning and data analysis make our lives much easier. Finding the right products is easier, navigating is easier, and finding new music is easier. This is all thanks to machine learning.

Image recognition

One of the applications of machine learning models is for sorting and classifying data. This type of classification can even be used for the classification of images. Search engines use this kind of algorithms to identify photos, and social media sites now use facial recognition to identify a person in a photo before the photo is even tagged. They do this by learning from data composed from other photos. If your social media account can recognize your face in a new photo, it's because it created models with data from all the other photos in your account.

Image recognition techniques require in-depth learning models. In-depth learning models are created with an artificial neural network, which will be discussed in more detail later in this book. Deep learning is the most complex type of machine learning where data is filtered through several hidden layers of nodes. They are called hidden layers because the models are unattended, which means that the features identified by the model are not pre-chosen by the data scientist. Usually the features are patterns that the model identifies on its own. Functions identified in neural networks can be quite complicated, the more complex the task, the more layers the model will have. Image sorting models may have only two or three layers, while self-driving cars have between one and two hundred hidden layers.

We have made great strides in this area in recent years due to the increased availability of computing power. Imagine the computing power needed to run thousands of data points through hundreds of stacked nodes at once. Deep learning and artificial neural networks have become more feasible over the past decade with the improvement of computers and the reduction of costs for processing large amounts of data. Certainly with the advent of the cloud, which gives data scientists access to enormous amounts of data without using physical storage space.

There is a website called ImageNet, a great resource for data scientists interested in photo classification and neural networks. ImageNet is a database of images that is publicly accessible for use in machine learning. The idea is that by making it publicly available, improving machine learning techniques will be a collaboration with data scientists around the world.

The ImageNet database has approximately 14 million photos in the database, with over 21,000 possible class groups. This offers a world of opportunities for data scientists to access and classify photos to learn and experiment with neural networks. Every year, ImageNet hosts a competition for data scientists worldwide to create new image classification models. The competition gets tougher every year. Now they are starting to move to classifying videos rather than images, which means that the complexity and required processing power will continue to grow exponentially. Using the millions of photos in the database, the ImageNet competition has made groundbreaking advances in image recognition in recent years.

Modern photo classification models require methods that can be classified very specifically. Even if two images have to be placed in the same category, they can look very different. How do you make a model that can distinguish them?

Take these two different photos of trees, for example. Ideally, if you were to create a neural network model that classified images of trees, you would want your model to categorize both as photos of trees. A person can recognize that these are both photos of trees, but the characteristics of the photo would make it very difficult to classify them with a machine learning model.

The less differences the variables have, the easier they can be classified. If all your photos of trees looked like the image on the left, with the tree in full view with all its features, the model would be easier to make. Unfortunately, this would lead to overfitting and when the model is presented with data with photos like the right, your model may not classify it correctly. We want our model to be able to classify our data even if they are not that easy to classify.

Incredibly, ImageNet has been able to create models that classify data with many variables and very similar data. Recently, they have created image recognition that can even identify and categorize photos with different dog breeds. Imagine all the variables and similarities that the model would need to recognize in order to properly see the difference between dog breeds.

The challenge of identifying similarities between a class is known as intra-class variability. If we have an image of a tree stump and a photo of a tree outlined in a field, we are dealing with variability within the class. This problem is how variables within the

the same class can differ, making it more difficult for our model to predict which category they will fall into. Most importantly, a lot of data is needed over time to improve the model and make it accurate.

To have an accurate model despite high levels of variability within the class, we will have to use additional techniques with our neural network models to find patterns between images. One method involves the use of convolutional neural networks. Instead of just having one model or algorithm, data is fed through several models stacked on top of each other. The neural networks convert image features into numerical values to sort them.

Unfortunately, it would be beyond the scope of this book to try to understand the way these deep neural networks work, but there are many books available that deal with these types of models and also include more extensive explanations of the coding required to perform this type of analysis. .

Voice recognition

Improvements in artificial intelligence have made speech recognition more recently very useful. Most of our smartphones now have a certain level of speech recognition, which means machine learning. Speech recognition takes the audio data we give it and turns it into text that can be interpreted.

The difficulty of speech recognition is the irregularities in the way people speak. Such as variability within the class. You and I may have different accents and different inflections that are difficult to explain when teaching a computer how to understand the human voice. If we both say the same word with different accents, how do we teach the model to understand us?

Speech recognition also uses neural networks to interpret data, such as image recognition. This is because the patterns in audio data are unlikely to be recognizable to a human. Data scientists use sampling to interpret data and make accurate predictions, despite the differences in people's voices. Sampling is done by measuring the height and length of the sound waves, which believe it may or may not be used to decipher what the user is saying. The recorded audio is converted into the wave map of frequencies. Those frequencies are
measured by numerical values and then passed through the hidden layers of the neural networks to search for patterns.

Medicine and medical diagnosis

Machine learning is not only useful for digital marketing or to get computers to respond to your requests. It also has the potential to improve the medical field, especially in the diagnosis of patients using data from previous patients.
With as much potential as machine learning has for medical diagnosis, it can be challenging to find patient data available for machine learning due to patient privacy laws. It is gradually gaining acceptance in the field of medicine, meaning data is becoming available to data scientists. Unfortunately, until now it has been difficult to have enough meaningful data to make models related to medical diagnosis. But the technology is there and available to use.
Machine learning can use image recognition to diagnose X-rays by bringing data from different patients to imaging scans to make predictions about new patients. Clustering and classification can be used to categorize different types of the same disease so that patients and medical professionals can better understand the variation of the same disease between two patients and their survival rate.

Medical diagnosis with machine learning can reduce doctors'
diagnosis errors or give doctors something to provide them
with a second opinion. It can also be used to predict the
likelihood of a positive diagnosis based on patient factors and
disease characteristics. One day, medical professionals may be
able to view data from thousands of patients about a
particular disease to make a new diagnosis.
But medical diagnosis is just one of many ways machine
learning can be used in medicine. Medical datasets remain
small today, and the science of machine learning still has a lot
of untapped potential in the field of medicine.

Stock forecasts

Stock traders look at many variables to decide what to do with
a stock whether they want to buy or sell or wait. They look at
certain features of a stock and trends in the market
environment to make an informed estimate of what to do. It
has been done this way for years. Brokers and traders had to
do manual research to make the best estimate.
Machine learning can now be used to do the same, except that
machine learning can be done much faster and more
efficiently. To be an effective trader you need to be able to
analyze trends in real time so you don't miss out on
opportunities. Machine learning can help traders find
agreements between stocks to make financial decisions using
statistical data.
Traders can use linear regression models to study data on
trends in past stock prices and what variables cause a stock
price to go up and down. They can use these regressions to
decide what to do with a stock.

Traders who want to analyze the performance of stocks often do this by using a so-called support vector machine. A supporting vector machine is a classification model in which data points are separated by a boundary line, with a category on one side and another category or another. Traders will use support vector machines to classify which stocks to buy and which stocks to sell. Using certain variables that should be indicative of the performance of a particular stock, that stock is placed on the side of the boundary line that indicates whether the price is likely to rise or fall.

Deep learning is also often used when making stock models. The hidden layers of a neural network can be helpful in identifying unseen trends or characteristics of a stock that could cause them to rise or fall in price.

There is no such thing as a certain bet or a risk-free investment. This was true when people made decisions, and it is still true when we use data science to make financial predictions. It is important to remember that investing in the stock market will always be risky. It is impossible to create a model that predicts anything reliable about the stock market. It is wild and unpredictable. But we have already learned that machine learning can find patterns that people may not be able to find on their own.

If you understand that stock market trends can be completely arbitrary and unpredictable, it is helpful to have another model that allows you to estimate the predictability of stocks. Knowing how accurate your predictions are for a given stock is just as important as the predictions themselves. Create a separate model to measure the predictability of a particular stock so you know how reliable your predictions are. Different stocks have different predictability levels. It is important to illustrate that with your model so that you can choose from the most reliable predictions.

Traders will proceed with the final decision on whether or not a stock will go up or down in value. But data science and machine learning can streamline the information analysis process that will aid the decision-making process. That's why you see more and more examples of machine learning models used when predicting inventory, and why at least familiarize yourself with the idea.

Learning associations

Marketers in all areas, from brick and mortar stores to online stores, are always looking for ways to connect products and increase sales. Whether you own a small bike shop or a huge online warehouse, finding patterns in your customer's buying behavior will help you make proactive decisions to boost sales and make more money.

Most of us will visit a supermarket during a certain week. Supermarkets are a perfect example of using product positioning to generate sales. Each supermarket will organize itself so that similar items are placed together. Baked goods have their own aisle, while fruits and vegetables have their place. They do this for two reasons; it makes it easier for the shopper to find what he needs and improves the customer experience. Product positioning can also help put customers in touch with products that they want to buy but weren't looking for when they first walked into the store.

In addition to placing the vegetables in the same aisle, there is yet another strategy that supermarkets can implement to lead customers to certain products. They can derive characteristics from a customer buying a specific product and use it to recommend other unrelated products. For example, you can assume that someone who buys fresh vegetables from the vegetable aisle will eat healthier. You can put vegetable smoothies in the same refrigerator where you store fruit. If a customer is looking for craft beer, you can tempt him with a snack and place the kettle chips on the same island as 12 packs of light beer.

If all that makes sense to you, you're on your way to understanding a technique called collaborative filtering. It is a machine learning technique widely used in internet marketing. If your search data shows that you have visited airline tickets to Cancun, you may see swimwear advertisements in your browser.

Marketing data scientists always try to answer this question; how can we use data to find a way to link a product to its target group? The point is to use data to link two otherwise unrelated products together to drive sales.

It is a way of making recommendations to a customer based on what you know about him. Machine learning can often find similarities or buying patterns with customers we may not have been looking for. This is a powerful marketing tool that is starting to emerge in modern times. Previously, most marketing agencies had to use intuition to find their target markets. Data scientists can now use quantitative data to paint a more accurate picture of their ideal customer. If you are interested in using machine learning in digital marketing, this is a subject you should know.

Collaborative filtering is different from just promoting a similar product to a customer. You make predictions about a customer's taste or preferences based on data you have collected from other customers. You base this prediction on a correlation you found between two products, and then a measure of the likelihood that product Y will be bought with product X. You use these estimates to decide what to market and to whom.

Spotify uses a similar process when making song recommendations. It uses data from all the music that you liked over time. If there is a connection between two artists, which means that many people have both artists in their library, the model can predict the probability that you will like the other artist.

The more products you have in your store, the more intensive it will be to find these correlations. In a perfect world, you will look for correlations between every different combination of products you have in your store.

This method of finding the probability that you like one product based on buying another product is called the Apiori algorithm. There are three criteria that must be met to confirm that there is a link between the two products and that you must somehow link them in your store. The first criterion is support. This gives you a measure of the popularity of a specific product. Of all your transactions, how often does this item appear in people's shopping cart?

The second part is confidence in the correlation between the two products. How likely are customers to buy a Y product when they buy an X product? After all, what is the lift of product Y? In other words, how likely someone is to buy Y with X based on the popularity of Y alone.

The model can also use data from things like purchases, social media engagements, etc. to make a prediction on the type of product you like. This sets it apart as machine learning rather than just data analysis because the model was looking for similarities, but the programmer didn't ask for a specific output. Perhaps there are certain features or characteristics of the group that the programmer is not even aware of. Perhaps unsupervised machine data tells that there is a high correlation between the two types of customers. These correlations take place all around us with similarities between groups of people. Sometimes a good computer model is needed to recognize the patterns in the data. Machine learning can find similarities that would be impossible to see without the help of computers and good models.

Data scientists in marketing industries are already using metrics to improve their stores online, and if you want to track online retailing, it's a good idea to start by reading about how data can help you identify similarities and trends across products, with machine learning as your tool.

Finance

The financial sector is seeing an increase in the use of machine learning. The use of data science and machine learning models makes the decision-making process faster and more efficient for financial institutions. The possibilities and applications of machine learning can be misunderstood, which means that it is often underutilized or misused in the financial sector.

Work that was once tedious and required hundreds of hours of human work can now be done by a computer in minutes. A well-known example is the use of machine learning for call center and customer service work. Many of the tasks that once required a human operator can now be accomplished over the phone with a robot designed with machine learning.

In addition to customer service, banks can now process and analyze contracts and financial information from thousands of customers that would otherwise be labor intensive - used to prepare credit reports and predict the likelihood of a customer defaulting on a loan. Machine learning techniques can view a history of a borrower's transactions before the bank decides whether to lend money to that person.

Machine learning is also used in fraud prevention. It has made the financial sector safer. Machine learning has improved the bank's ability to detect patterns in transactions indicative of fraud. Rather than being assigned people to track the transaction and look for signs of fraud, machine learning models can learn from fraud data to find patterns by automatically searching millions of customer transactions.

Spam detection

A well-known example of a relatively simple machine learning tool is spam detection. If we use guided learning and define the variables that are relevant, the model will have certain characteristics to look for in received email messages. The model may search for certain keywords or phrases to detect whether an email is spam or not. Words like "buy" or "save" can let your inbox know when you receive spam email. The problem with this method is that in many cases there is not always spam. There may be other keywords or phrases that we would overlook.

This is where strengthening learning comes in handy. There are so many features that can be an indication of spam email, and some of them we might not even be able to explain. Reinforcement learning will make it possible to find these patterns independently, without explicit guidance. Instead, we tell the model when it has correctly identified spam. Sometimes we find in our inbox an email message that the model has not classified as spam, so we manually move it to our spam folder. Now the model knows that this message is spam, and this piece of data is added to the model to improve the forecast next time. So over time, the machine gets better the more relevant data it gets.

This type of machine learning is known as classification. Our output falls into separate categories. In statistics, discrete variables are variables that can be identified in only a finite number of categories. An example of a discrete variable is the number of cars a car dealer sells in a week. It is discreet because the car dealer cannot sell half a car. The variable must be an integer.

Introduction to statistics

Statistics is the mathematical science of data. It is a practice of collecting, observing, and analyzing data to derive meaning and explore quantifiable relationships between different variables. Machine learning is a form of inferential statistics, which means that by investigating the relationship between variables, we must be able to make predictions for new variables.

Statistics are used in a wide variety of disciplines. It is used in biology to study and investigate the life of animals and plants. It has broad applications in business, from making stock market forecasts to analyzing consumer behavior. Economists use statistics to explain quantifiable patterns in world markets. In medicine, statistics can be used to improve the way doctors and disease specialists view the spread and prevention of diseases.

Statistics are at the heart of machine learning. If you're not willing to dive into statistics, machine learning is not for you. Machine learning uses statistical algorithms to help computers learn. Machine learning is all about tracking data and how computers can use data to improve themselves.

There are two types of statistics relevant to this book. The first is a descriptive analysis, which you can use at the beginning of your modeling process to look for indicators in your data. But most of what we do in machine learning falls into another category called predictive analysis.

Important term; Descriptive analysis. The descriptive analysis helps us to investigate that we are now. Looking at our current situation in the context of the past and seeing why things are the way they are. Why do some things sell better than others? What trends do we see in products currently on the market?

Important term; Predictive analysis. Predictive analysis helps us to see and understand what will happen in the future based on the current indicators. When we use machine learning for predictive analysis, it is important that we stay current and continue to provide the model with new data. Which trends should we look out for?

Machine learning is just another way of understanding the data around us and helping us understand our present and predict the future. But it requires past and present data so we can find trends and see where they can lead.

Within statistics, there are two overarching categories of data that we will use, and all of our data will somehow fall into one category or the other.

The first category is quantitative data. Quantitative data is data that can be measured with a numerical value. Some examples of quantitative data are length, income or the square footage of a house. All these variables can be measured by a certain number, making them quantitative.

The second category is qualitative data. Qualitative data is data where the variables are assigned to categories or classes. Examples of qualitative data include a person's gender, blood type, whether a property has a pool or not. This data can be sorted by identity and is non-numeric. Therefore it is qualitative.

Quantitative data can be discrete or continuous. If we have a data set with a variable that records the number of patients a hospital had last year, it would be considered discrete.

Discrete variables have a finite amount of values they can have, and they are always whole numbers. It is impossible to have half a patient or a percentage of a patient. Therefore, this variable is discrete.

Data can also be continuous. An example of continuous data is an income variable. Income can take half values, and there are almost endless possibilities for the value of income in data.

Some other important terms to remember are the mean, median, and mode. You will often hear these three things referred to in this book when we talk about regressions. These are all different degrees of central tendency. The mean is our mean value for data. If we have a variable for a person's age, we find the average of the age by adding up all ages and then dividing by the number of respondents in a dataset.

The median is the value in the middle of the dataset. If you had taken all the answers by age and found the answer right in the middle of a sorted list of answers, this would be your median.

The mode is the most common answer. If we took a sample of the ages of eleven people and found that the ages were 19, 19, 20, 21, 22, 22, 22, 23, 24, 24, 25, the mode would be 22 because it is the most occurs in this example. The median would also be 22 because it is in the middle of this sorted list of responses. When creating a statistical model, there are many important terms related to the accuracy of our models. The most important and most mentioned in this book are bias and variance. These are different types of prediction errors that can occur when we create statistical models. Ideally, we want to minimize the prevalence of bias and variance in our models. They will always be there, and as a data scientist, you need to find the right balance of bias and variance in your models, whether by choosing different data or using different types of models. There are many ways to reduce variance and bias within a model, depending on what you are trying to do with the data. By reducing this with the wrong approach, you run the risk that your model will be mounted too much or too little. If your model is biased, it means that the average difference between your predictions and actual values is very high.

Variance is how we can spread our predicted data points. Usually, the variance results from overfitting on the sample data we used to create the model. It does not accurately predict the outcome of new variables.

Errors will always occur in your models. It is a fact of life that no matter how well you predict something, there is always a random or non-random variation in the universe that makes your prediction slightly different from the actual outcome.

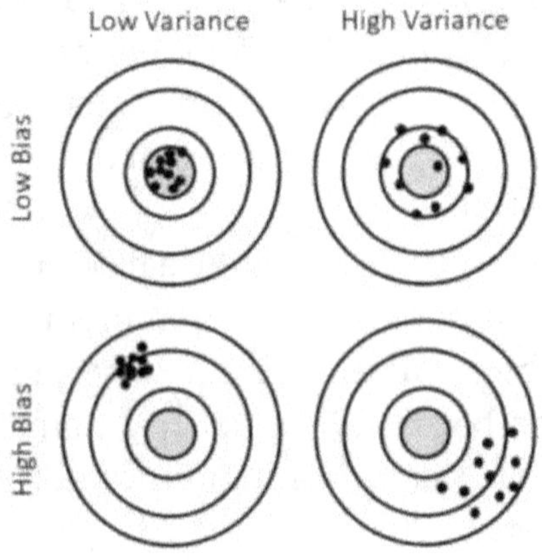

I made a visual example of four bullseye targets to illustrate the difference between high bias and variance models. In this case, the center of the bullseye represents the true value that our model is trying to predict. The top left corner is the ideal model. Note that all of our predicted data points hit the bull's eye. This model is quite accurate and puts our predicted data points around the true value. This is due to a low variance; a lack of "staggered" data points and a low bias; substantiation that distorts our results.

In the top right target, the model suffers from high variance. You can see that our data points are grouped around the bullseye. Unfortunately, the average distance between the predicted values and the bullseye is high due to the large variance.

In the lower left target, the model did not suffer much from high variance. The average distance between the predicted data points is low, but they are not clustered around the bullseye, but slightly off due to high bias. This is likely due to insufficient training data, which means that the model will not perform well when introduced into new data.

The bottom right model has both a high variance and a high bias. In this worst case scenario, the model is very inaccurate because the average distance between predicted data points and the actual value is high and the predicted data points are skewed.

Variance can be caused by a significant degree of correlation between variables. Using too many independent variables can also be a cause of the high variance. Sometimes, if the variance is too great, we can combat that by allowing a small amount of bias in the model. This is known as regularization. We will discuss that a little later.

In statistics, the population is the group of people or dataset you are trying to analyze. The sample is the subgroup of that population, whose data you use to create your model. The parameters are characteristic of the population variables you are trying to identify and make predictions in your model.

Descriptive statistics are the use of data to study a population. Descriptive statistics typically include the mean or average, mode, media, size, correlation. Machine learning falls into the category of inferential statistics because we use the data to find patterns and relationships, but also to make predictions based on this information. Inferential statistics or descriptive statistics use the characteristics of your population to make predictions. This is where your regression models and classification models come in. When we derive something, we make a logical conclusion about a population and the knowledge we gain.

If you look at data, also pay attention to the distribution. This is how the data is distributed in our chart. It shows the frequency of values of our data and how they appear in combination with each other.

We use our variance to find the standard deviation. Standard deviation is the average of the distances between the predicted data points and the real data points on a regression or prediction model.

We also need to make sure that we are aware of models that suffer from over- and underfitting. An overfitted model is good at predicting results using the training data, but if you are introducing new data, it will be difficult. It is like a model that remembers instead of learns. It can happen if you don't use random data in your training sample.

Underfitting describes a model that is too simple and does not investigate significant data patterns. It may predict well, but the variables and parameters are not specific enough to give us meaningful insights if you don't have enough training data, your model may not fit.

One of the most common mistakes when looking at data is confusing correlation with causality. If I told you that every person who killed last year laid eggs every week, I couldn't claim that people who buy eggs are murderers. Maybe I look at my data and see an increase in the number of people buying milk as well as an increase in teenage pregnancies. Could I argue that there is a connection between people who drink a lot of milk and teenage pregnancies? Or teens who got pregnant caused people to buy more milk.

This is the difference between correlation and causation. Sometimes the data shows trends that appear to be related. When two events are correlated, it means that they seem to have a relationship because they move along the graph on a similar trajectory and in a similar space over time. While causality means that the relationship between the two events causes one event that causes another.

A number of criteria must be met to suggest that two cases are causally related. The first is covariation. The causal variable, and the event, should have created the need to be covariant, meaning that a change in one leads to a change in the other. The second criterion to be met is that the causative event must occur before the event that it should have caused. For an event to be considered causal, it must first come.

Third, the data scientist should check for external factors. To make it clear that one causes the other; you must be able to demonstrate that the other variables of the event are not the real cause. If the causal variable still creates the effect even when other variables are considered, you can argue that there is a causal relationship.

Choosing the right type of model for machine learning

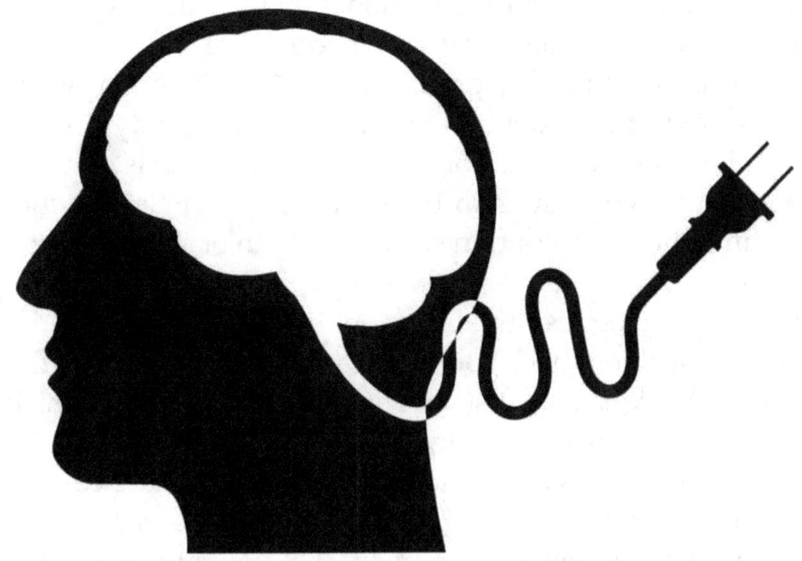

Imagine yourself as a carpenter. What kind of tools do you think you have loaded in your truck when you arrive at a workplace? You will likely have a hammer and a drill, as well as a few different types of saws. You probably have a few planes and a good set of drills. If you know how to do your job, you will know when you will know the purpose of each of these tools and when to use them all. Each of these tools has a specific purpose. The drill cannot do the work of a hammer, nor would you attempt to cut anything with a hammer.
A data scientist who wants to do machine learning has their own set of tools, each with a different purpose and designed for a different function. Depending on the type of data you use and what you want to know, you have to choose different algorithmic models to do the job.

Statistical algorithms can serve different purposes. Some predict a value; as a regression model that predicts your income base based on your years of education and work experience. Some models predict the probability of an event, such as a medical model that predicts the probability that a patient will survive a year or two, etc. Other models sort things by placing them in different categories or classes, such as sorting photo recognition software photo of different types of dogs.

Depending on the result you are looking for, you will need your statistical tool belt. You must familiarize yourself with the technical skills of statistics. You also need to know which tool to use and when to use it. Here I have made an extensive list of the different types of statistical models that are common in machine learning. To be able to write the code to build these models yourself, I recommend that you take some time to study in the programming language you have chosen. But this list gives you an introductory understanding of each type of model and when they are useful.

In order for machine learning to be effective, you need to choose the right model and the model that works best and have relevant data for the model and demand.

Today, especially when using the Internet and digital marketing, there are certain questions that cannot be properly understood without the use of data and machine learning that can analyze it. Machine learning and data science allow you to track your customers and their buying habits so you can better adapt to their needs as they change.

The better you interpret your data, the easier it is to identify trends and patterns, so you can anticipate the next change. Machine learning can be divided into three different categories, each with different unique algorithms serving different purposes. For starters, we'll talk about the differences between guided, uncontrolled, and reinforcing learning.

Learning under supervision

Programmers use labeled data in supervised learning. Before we start using the algorithms, the data we look at is already predetermined. We know the inputs and outputs we are looking for. X and Y. We are trying to find a relationship between X and Y that we have chosen.

After you find a relationship between X and Y, you get a model that predicts a result based on the relationships your machine has observed in the data. Guided learning is used for regression and classification models. In machine learning, we refer to characteristics as a certain measurable property or characteristic of the data.

The first type of guided learning we will talk about and the first type of statistical model is called regression. Regression is a model in which data input and output are continuous. There are different types of regression, but the most basic form is linear regression. We use linear regression to find a relationship between an input X and an output Y. Once we have estimated this relationship, we can predict Y with X. Linear models can, and usually have, more than one X. In regression ; output Y has a numerical value.

Regression analysis

Regression is the simplest type of machine learning; this is usually where you start when you first learn how to use your data. You have a set of X values and you want to study their relationship to Y, the output. Our independent variables, the X's in our model, gain weight and for each value of X it is multiplied by the weight until the concatenated function creates a prediction for Y.

We can create a predictive model for Y using data we already know the X and Y for. If we bring this information back, we get the weights of X. If we have enough relevant data, we can eventually predict Y and be unfamiliar with known values for X.

We draw our known Y and X values on a scatter plot, and our regression model finds the "best fit" line through the data points. The regression line is called a hyperplane. The slope of the line is called the slope.

We can measure the distance between the predicted value and the actual data point, and we call this measurement deviation. Our goal in creating a linear regression is to minimize the deviation in our predictions. The smaller the difference, the deviation, the more accurate your model.

Most statistical models used in machine learning are rooted in this first algorithm. Create a model that predicts a result by plotting our data points along a line or in clusters. But the line isn't always straight and sometimes the line doesn't show us the best fit.

An example of a non-linear regression function is the Sigmoid function. The Sigmoid function creates an S-shaped curve. Rather than predict a value, the Sigmoid function takes independent variables and produces a probability between one and zero.

Simple linear regression. In simple linear regression, we study the relationship between some predicted value Y and some predictor X. We call our Y the dependent variable because it depends on the value of X. Our X is known as the independent variable.

If you took algebra or pre-calculus in high school or college, you may remember that the equation was a line;

$$Y = mX + b$$

If you were to draw this equation, you would have a graph that looks something like this:

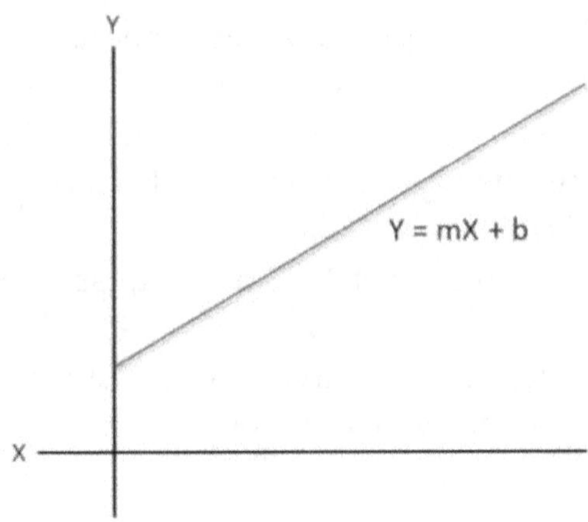

As you can see, the line shows that for each value of X there is a different value of Y. You can predict the value of Y for each new value of X. In this graph, the value of Y increases as the value of X increases. This is not always the case.

This is the most simplistic regression, but it is important to understand how it works, as we will continue to build on it from now on. Most of the statistical analysis involves a plot as shown above, which predicts an output dependent variable based on an input, the independent variable. This is an example of guided learning because we specify the Y variable and the X variable we use before we start modeling.

With almost all predictions, there will be more than one independent variable that will determine our dependent variable. This brings us to our next type of regression.

Multiple linear regression. In data science and most statistics tasks, this is the most popular type of regression. With multiple linear regression we have one output variable Y as before. However, the difference now is that we will have multiple X's or independent variables that will predict our Y.

An example of using multiple linear regression to predict the price of real estate apartments in New York City. Our Y or dependent variable is the price of an apartment in New York City. The price is determined by X, our independent variables such as square meters, distance to transport, number of rooms.

If we were to write this as an expression, it would look something like this:

apt_price = $\beta 0$ + $\beta 1$ square feet + $\beta 2$ dist_transport + $\beta 3$ num_rooms

We take sample data, data we already have where we know our X's and their Y's and we view them in a graph like this:

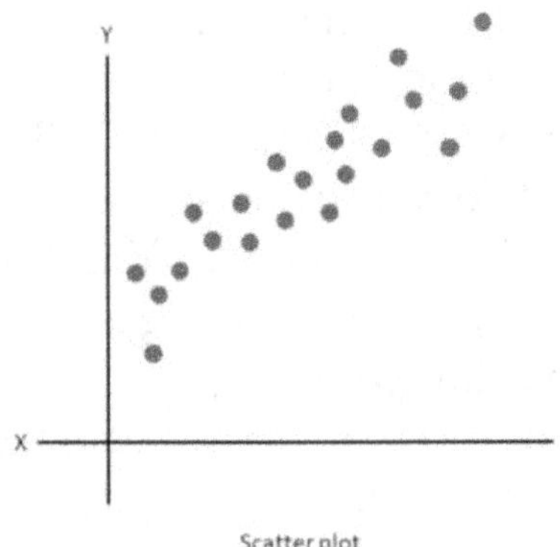

Scatter plot

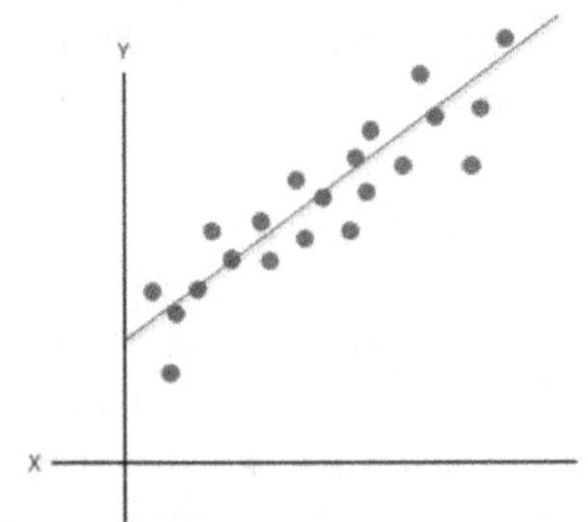

$apt\_price = \beta_0 + \beta_1\ sq\_foot + \beta_2\ dist\_transport + \beta_3\ num\_rooms$

You can see that the values of X and Y don't create a perfect line, but there is a trend. We can use that trend to make predictions about future values of Y. So we create a multilinear regression and end with a line going through the center of our data points. This is called the best fit line and it is how we will predict our Y when we get new X values in the future.

The difference here is that instead of writing m for slope, we wrote β. This comparison is much the same as if I had written Y = b + m1X1 + m2x2 + m3x3

Except now we have labels and we know what our X's and our Y's are. If you see a multi-line equation in the future, it will most likely be written in this form. Our β is what we call a parameter. It is like a magic number that tells us what effect the value of our X has on the Y. Each independent variable has a unique parameter. We find the parameters by making a regression model. Over time, with machine learning, our model will be exposed to more and more data, improving our parameter and making our model more accurate.

We can make the model by using training data with the actual price of New York City apartments and the actual input variables of square meters, distance to transportation and many rooms. Our model 'learns' to approximate the price based on real data. Then, when we connect the independent variable for an apartment with an unknown price, our model can predict what the price will be.

This is guided learning using a linear regression model. It is checked because we tell the model what answer we want it to give us; the price of apartments in New York City. It learns how to more accurately predict the price as it gets more data and we continue to evaluate its accuracy.

Ordinary least squares OLS will try to find a regression line that minimizes the sum of squared errors

Polynomial regression. Our next type of regression is called a polynomial regression. In the last two types of regression, our models created a straight line. This is because the relationship between our X and Y is linear, which means that the effect X has on Y does not change if the value of X changes. In polynomial regressions, our model results in a line with a curve.

If we tried to use linear regression to fit a graph that has nonlinear features, we would do badly to make the best fit line. Take the graph on the left, for example; the scatter plot has an upward trend as before, but with a curve. In this case, a straight line does not work. Instead, with a polynomial regression we will make a line with a curve corresponding to the curve in our data, like the graph on the right

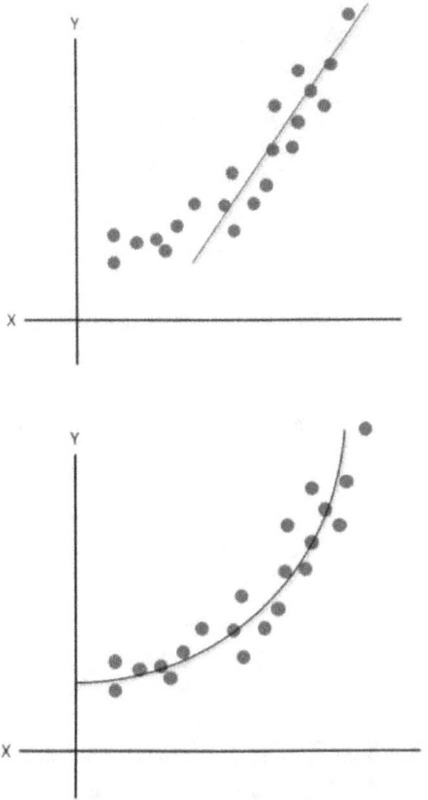

The equation of a polynomial will look like the linear equation, with the difference that there will be a polynomial expression on one or more of our X values. For example:

$$Y = mX2 + b$$

The effect X has on Y changes exponentially as the value for X changes.

Vector regression support. This is another important tool for data scientists and one that you should familiarize yourself with. It is most commonly used in case of classification. The idea here is to find a line through a space that separates data points into different classes. Vector regression support is another type of guided learning. It is also used for regression analysis. It is a type of binary classification technique that is not related to probability.

To support Vector Regression, all your training data falls into one category or the other. You want to know in which category a new data point falls. Your data is separated by a hyperplane into these two classes. When creating a model for

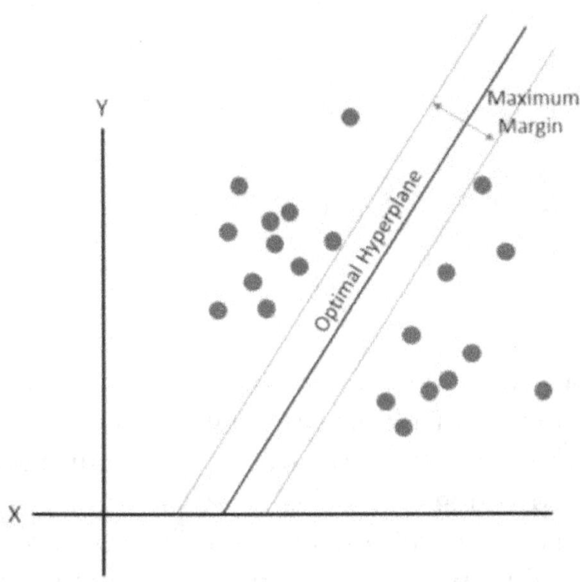

the hyperplane, try to find a hyperplane that maximizes the distance between the two classes. For example, in the following image, you have a scatter plot where the data points can be divided into two different classes. In this case, lines one and three can separate the data points into two separate classes. For your model, however, you should choose rule two because it maximizes the margin between the two classes so they are clearer. The larger the margin, the better.

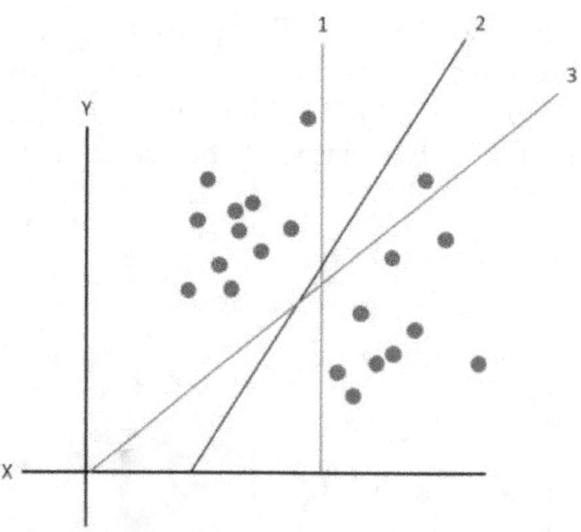

Ridge regression. This is a technique often used to analyze data suffering from multicollinearity. Using cam regression correctly can reduce standard errors and make your model more accurate depending on the characteristics of your data. Ridge regression can be useful when your data contains independent variables with a high correlation. If you can predict an independent variable by using another independent variable, your model runs the risk of multicollinearity. For example, if you use variables that measure a person's height and weight; these variables probably create multicollinearity in the model. Multicollinearity can affect the accuracy of your predictions. Consider the type of predictive variables you use to avoid multicollinearity. The type of data you use, as well as the collection method, can cause multicollinearity. Chances are you have not selected a wide range of independent variables. Your data points may look too similar because your choice of independent variables is limited.

Multicollinearity can also be caused by too specific a model. You have more variables than data points. If you have decided to use a linear model, which has aggravated multicollinearity, you can try applying a cam regression technique.

Ridge regression works by allowing a little bit of bias in the model to make your predictions more accurate. This technique is also known as regularization.

Another method is to improve the accuracy of the model by standardizing independent variables. The simplest way is to change the coefficients of some independent variables to zero to reduce complexity. However, we will not simply set them to zero, but standardization implements a system that rewards coefficients closer to zero. This reduces the coefficients, which reduces the complexity of the model, but the independent variables remain in the model. This will give the model more bias, but it is a tradeoff for more accurate predictions.

LASSO regression. LASSO regression is another 'shrinkage' technique. A very similar approach to ridge regression in that it encourages leaner, simpler prediction models. In lasso regression, the model is a bit stricter about lowering the value of coefficients. LASSO stands for the least absolute crimp and selection operator.

Data on our scatter plot is reduced to a more compact point, such as the average of the data. Like ridge regression, we use this when the model suffers from multicollinearity.

ElasticNet regression. ElasticNet regression works by combining the techniques of LASSO and ridge regression. The main goal is to try to improve the LASSO regression. It is a combination of both methods for rewarding lower coefficients in LASSO and Ridge regression. All three of these models are accessible via the glmnet package in R and Python.

Bayesian regression. Bayesian regression models are useful when we have insufficient data or data with poor distribution. These types of regressions are made with probability distributions instead of data points, which means that the graph will appear as a bell curve representing the variance with the most common values in the center of the curve.

In Bayesian regression, the dependent variable Y is not a value but a probability. Instead of trying to predict a value, we try to predict the probability of an outcome. This is known as frequentistic statistics and Bayes' theorem forms the basis for this type of statistics. Frequent statistics suggest whether something will happen and the probability that it will.

When we talk about frequentistic statistics, we also include conditional probability. Conditional probability involved events the outcomes of which depend on each other. Every time you throw a coin it is an independent event, which means that the previous coin toss does not change the chance of the next coin toss. Throwing a toss is therefore not a conditional opportunity.

Events can also be dependent, which means that the previous event can change the probability of the next event. Say I had a bag of marbles and I wanted to know how likely it is to get different colors out of the bag. If I have a bag with 3 green marbles and 3 red marbles, and I draw a red marble, the chance of drawing a red marble decreases on my next draw. This would be an example of conditional probability.

Decision trees

One of the models that we will discuss later is called neural networks. They are the most advanced forms of machine learning and are used for many different purposes. I've associated this with decision trees because of how often people turn to neural networks for classification problems when much simpler models are available. Decision trees and the related random forest models can be just as useful. Despite the power of neural networks, they cannot be used for everything. Fortunately, we have options, and the purpose of this book is to know what your options are if you decide to build a model. The next place to look when neural networks don't work are decision trees. Decision trees divide data into subcategories with decision and leaf nodes in the form of a tree.

Decision trees have a number of advantages over neural networks (discussed later in this chapter). For starters, neural networks need huge amounts of data and powerful computers to process them. The advantage of using a decision tree is that they are relatively straightforward, especially if you compare them to neural networks. Unlike most models in this book, they are very easy to read a decision tree, even for the untrained eye. This makes them a good candidate when choosing a model to be presented to stakeholders.

Decision trees are another form of guided learning, which means that we label the categories we want to sort before creating the model. In some cases, decision trees can complete regression tasks, but most often they are used as classification models. When decision trees are used for regression, the leaf nodes end in probabilities.

Decision trees start with a so-called root knot at the top of the tree. Then the root node is split into two nodes after the root node. Nodes are individual leaves in the tree, and the middle nodes are where decisions are made, known as the decision nodes. The decision tree ends at the bottom in what is called a terminal node, at the bottom of a branch, where the decision is completed.

Ideally, the decision tree sorts the data quickly, layer by layer. That's why we call the model "greedy" because the top nodes try to sort the data as quickly as possible, so fewer layers are needed. Like neural networks, decision trees often suffer from overfitting. A decision tree usually does not work with other datasets because the sorting is so specific to each dataset.

Below is an example of a decision tree about whether or not to assign an applicant to the applicant, determined by qualification factors. The basic node is whether or not the

a
r
a
c
v
t

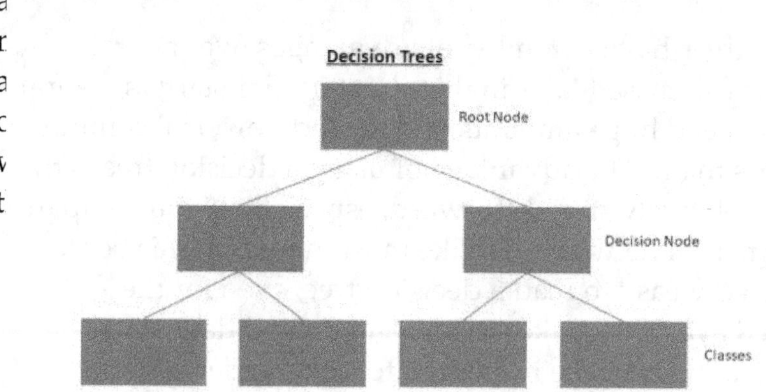

Random forests

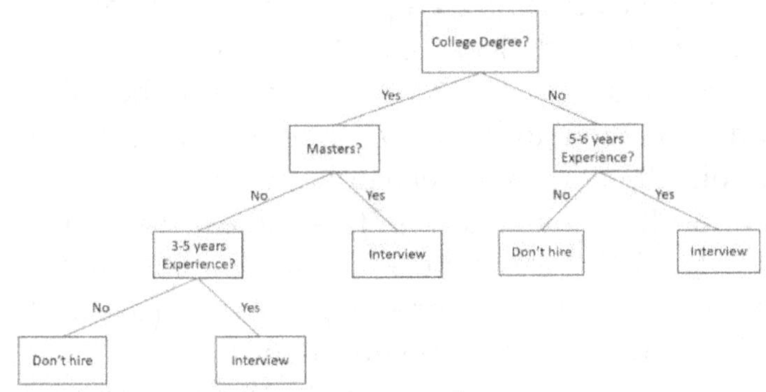

Using only one decision tree on your model can limit the categories in which the data is split and the outcome of the decisions. Because the decision trees are "greedy", this means that certain categories are chosen to sort, which means that other categories cannot be chosen either. But there is an easy way around that. One way to diversify your decision trees and improve the accuracy of your model is to use random forests.

If a real forest consists of several trees, that is exactly what a random forest is. Instead of having just one decision tree, split the data into several decision trees. If you only have one tree, models can often suffer from large variance. Creating a random forest is a way to combat that in your model. It is one of the best tools available for data mining. Any forest is as close as possible to a prepackaged algorithm for data mining purposes.

In a random forest, all trees work together. The overall result of all trees is usually correct, even if a few trees end with poor predictions. To make the final forecast, the results of all trees are added together. Using votes from the mean values of all trees gives us a definitive prediction.

Since we use comparable data, there is a risk of correlation between the trees if they all try to do the same. If we use trees that are less correlated, the model performs better.

Imagine if we bet on a coin flip. We have a hundred dollars each and there are three choices. I can flip the coin once and the winner of that toss can keep $ 100. Or I can flip the coin ten times and we bet ten dollars every time. The third option is to flip the coin 100 times and bet a dollar on every roll. The real expected result of any version of this game is the same. But if you've done 100 tosses, you're less likely to lose all your money than if you've only done one toss. Data scientists call this method bootstrapping. It is the machine-student equivalent of diversifying a stock portfolio. We want to have a model that gives us an accurate prediction. The more we split our decision trees, the more accurate our data will be. But it is important that the individual trees have little correlation with each other. The trees in the forest must be diverse.

How do we prevent correlation in a random forest? Each tree first takes a random sample from the dataset, so that each tree has a slightly different set of data from each other. The tree chooses a trait that creates the most separation between nodes, in a greedy process, just like individual trees. However, in any forest, trees can only choose certain elements from the general group of elements, so each tree is separated by different elements.

So the trees are not correlated because they use different functions to make decisions about classification. In any forest, it is best to use at least 100 trees to get an accurate view of the data, depending on the dataset you are working with. In general, the more trees you have, the less your model will become overfit. Random learning in a forest is called a "low-supervision technique" because our outcome has been chosen and we can see the sorting method, but it is up to each tree to categorize and separate variables by attributes.

Classification models will tell us in which category something falls. The categories are initially defined by the programmer. An example of a classification model that any forest could use would be a model that determines whether incoming emails should place spam in your "inbox" or "spam" folder.

To create the model, we create two categories that our Y can fall into; spam and not spam. We program the model to search for keywords or a specific email address that may indicate spam. The presence of words such as "buy" or "offer" will help the model determine whether the email falls into the spam category or not. The algorithm records data and learns over time by comparing its predictions to the actual value of the output. Over time, it makes minor adjustments to its model, making the algorithm more efficient over time.

Classifications

A few times in this book we have referred to classification models. Some of the models we have already mentioned can be classified, but the following are more supervised learning models used specifically for classification.

Classification requires labeled data and creates discontinuous predictions. The graphs are non-linear for classification problems. There can be two classes in a classification problem, or even more. Classification models are probably the most widely used part of machine learning and data science.

The first type of classification is binary classification. In binary classification, the data is classified into two categories, labeled 1 or 0. We call it binary classification because there are only two possible categories, and all of our data falls into one or the other.

But there are cases where we have more than two categories and for this we use multi-class classification models. We also have linear decision boundaries, separating data on either side of a line. Not all data can be classified on both sides of a decision boundary.

The first image shows an example of a classification with a linear decision boundary. In the second image, there are almost two classes, but they cannot be separated linearly. In the third image, data points are mixed and linear boundary classification is not possible. Depending on the type of data you use, there are different model choices that are better suited for different tasks

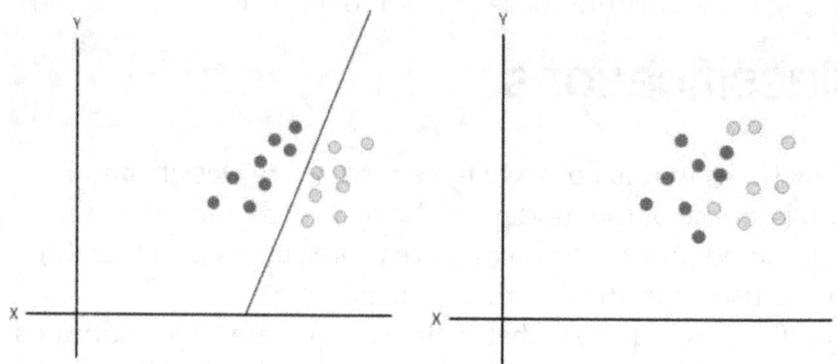

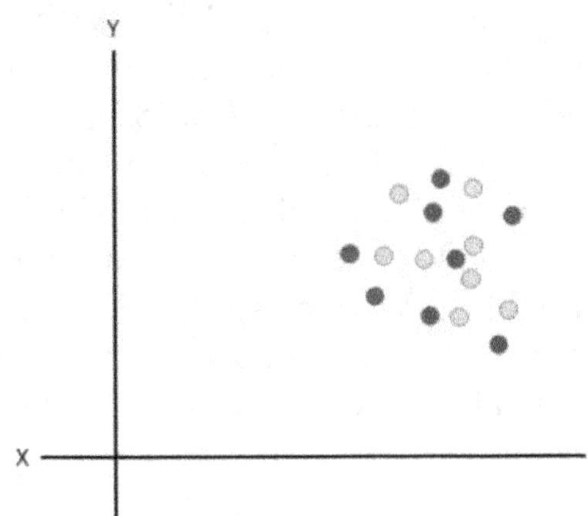

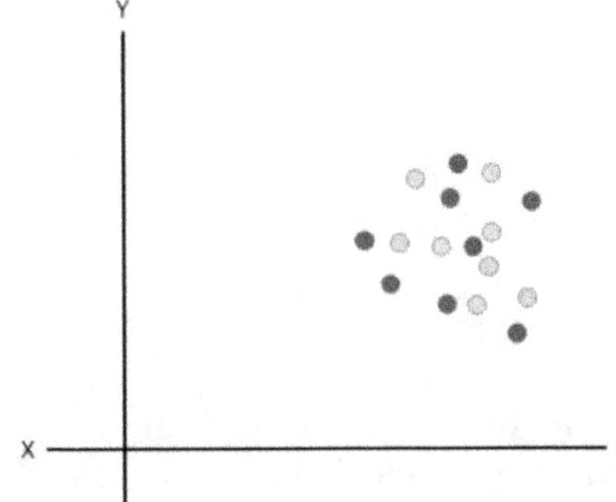

Logistic regression / classification

This method is used to classify dependent and categorical variables. Logistic regression calculates probabilities based on independent variables. It values the variables "Yes or No" to sort them. Usually used with binary classification.
If you cannot separate the data into classes using a linear boundary, as in the examples above, this is the method to use. It is one of the most common types of machine learning algorithms. Not only does it sort into categories, but it also tells us the probability that a category exists.
We denote this model by taking the odds function, where p is the probability of an event;

$$\frac{p}{1 - p}$$

And creating a formula called the logit

$$\log\frac{p}{1 - p}$$

K Nearest neighbors

K closest neighbors are one of the simplest and most widely used data classification methods. It is a form of supervised learning that is used for both classification and regression, and it is also the most basic clustering algorithm. Simply put, it's about taking a data point and placing it with the most common and nearest group on the scatter plot.

In KNN a new data point is classified based on the average median value of its neighbors K. The nearest neighbors of a new data point 'vote' for which classification it falls. K is the number of nearest neighbors who vote in the model. Set k to a number - this is the number of nearest data points that the new data point will analyze to choose which point it fits. The proximity of data points is measured using an Euclidean distance.

Take the following two images as an example. We have split our data into two classifications; the white dots and the black dots. A new data point is introduced, the triangle, and we would like to predict which classification it belongs to.

In this model we chose K = 4. If you choose k = 4, the four closest data points are analyzed. The most common class among the adjacent data points is the class in which the new data point will be placed. In this case, you can see in the image on the right that the four white dots are the closest classification. Therefore, the new data point is classified in that class.

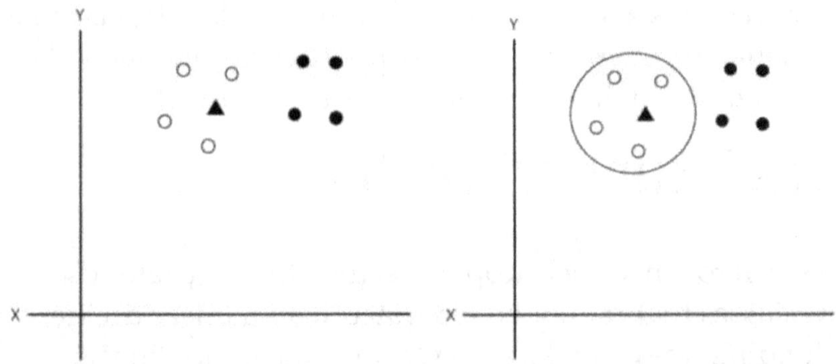

There are a few factors to consider when choosing the value for k. The higher the number for k, the closer we get to the true classification of our new data point. There is an optimal point where the value of k must stop rising to avoid overfitting.

If you choose to use a number for K that is too low, chances are your model will have a high degree of bias. If you use too high a number, the computational power required to calculate the value is too expensive. You may consider using an odd number when choosing a value for K, rather than an even number. Using an odd number is less likely to encounter a draw between classes that vote for a data point. Data scientists often choose the number 5 as the default for k.

Using a large number for K will be very data intensive. Large datasets are also difficult to use with KNN machine learning models. If you are using larger data sets, you need to calculate the distance between hundreds or perhaps thousands of data points. It also does not perform well when you use this method on a model that exists in more than two dimensions. Again, it has to do with the computing power required to calculate this distance between many data points.

Vector support

Support vector is another type of classifier. It classifies using a hyperplane. In general, we use a support vector model with smaller data sets, where it performs reasonably well.

Kernel Support vector

While we'll touch kernel support vectors, they are later used to sort classes that cannot be separated with a linear divider. The dividing line can take many forms (linear, nonlinear, polynomial, radial, sigmoid).

Remind the classification of a linear boundary we just talked about, with the classification looking something like the following image:

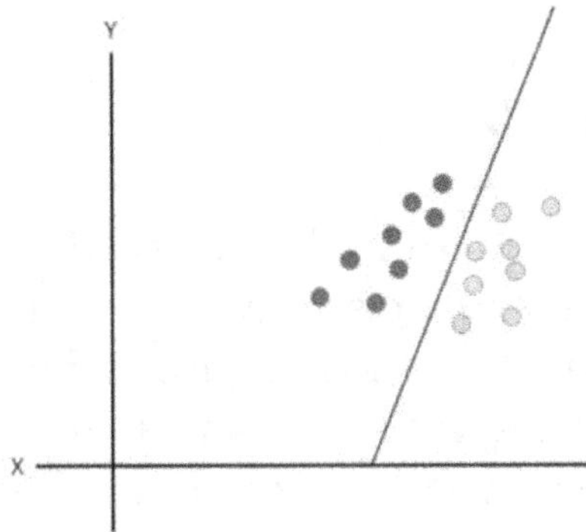

In this image, our data can be classified by a straight line separating the two different data categories. It would be helpful if data can always be separated in this way, but unfortunately, in fact, it's not always that neat and tidy, usually you will have to separate the data in a way that looks

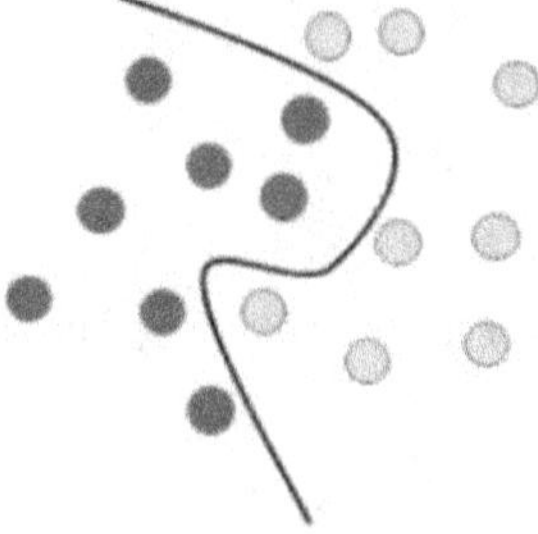

more like this:

In this example, the data cannot be separated by a linear boundary line. So instead we have to use a technique called the kernel trick. It uses a measure of agreement between data points to classify them.

Naive Bayes

Think of Bayes' theorem from the first section on guided learning. Naïve Bayes models assume that predictors are independent. This model is easy to use and useful in large data sets. It is often used to sort spam emails.
We use Baye's rule here. The idea of Bayes Rule is that by adding new, relevant information to what we already know, we can update our knowledge based on that new information. If we wanted to know the chance of rain falling this afternoon, we can find out what percentage of the days it rains per year. But then we found out it was raining this morning. How do you think this affects the chance of rain this afternoon?
So our ability to predict the probability of something will improve as we receive more information about the event.

$$P(A \mid B) = \frac{P(B \mid A)P(A)}{P(B)}$$

Mathematically, Bayes' theorem is expressed as follows:

So we can classify new data points using Bayes' theorem. The way it works is when we get a new data point, we calculate the probability that that data point falls into a category based on the characteristics of that data point.

Learning without supervision

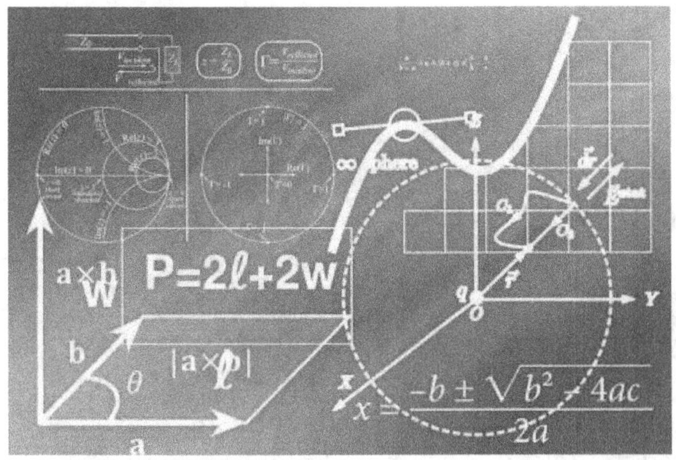

Unattended machine learning uses untagged data. Data scientists do not yet know the output. The algorithm must discover patterns itself, where patterns would otherwise be unknown. Find a structure in a place where the structure is otherwise imperceptible. The algorithm independently finds data segments. The model looks for patterns and structure in an otherwise unlabeled and unrecognizable mass of data. Unsupervised learning allows us to find patterns that would not be observable without computer scientists. Sometimes huge data sets have patterns and it is impossible to search them all to find trends.

This is good for researching consumer buying behavior so that you can group customers into categories based on patterns in their behavior. The model may discover that there are similarities in buying patterns between different subsets of a market, but if you did not have your model to search through these vast amounts of complicated data, you will never realize the nature of these patterns. The beauty of unsupervised learning is the ability to discover patterns or features in vast amounts of data that you wouldn't be able to identify without the help of your model.

A good example of unsupervised learning is fraud detection. Fraud can be a major problem for financial companies, and with large amounts of daily users, it can be difficult for companies to identify fraud without the help of machine learning tools. Models can learn to recognize fraud as tactics change with technology. To tackle new, unknown fraud techniques, you must use a model that can detect fraud under unique circumstances.

It is better to have more data when detecting fraud. Fraud detection services should use a range of machine learning models to effectively fight fraud. Use of both supervised and non-supervised models. It is estimated that approximately $ 32 billion in fraudulent credit card activity will take place next year, by 2020 fraud detection models will classify the output (credit card transactions) as legitimate or fraudulent.

They can be classified based on a function such as the time of day or the location of the purchase. If a trader usually sells around $ 20 and suddenly has a sale for $ 8000 from a foreign location, the model will most likely classify this trade as fraudulent.

The challenge of using machine learning for fraud detection is that most transactions are not fraudulent. If there were even a significant number of fraudulent transactions among non-fraudulent transactions, credit cards would not be a viable sector. The percentage of fraudulent card transactions is so small that it can create models that are skewed that way. The $ 8,000 purchase in a strange location is suspect, but is the result of a traveling cardholder rather than fraudulent activity. Unattended learning makes it easier to identify suspicious buying patterns such as strange shipping locations and random jumps in user reviews.

Clustering

Clustering is a subgroup of unsupervised learning. Clustering is the task of grouping similar things. When we use clustering, we can identify attributes and sort our data based on those attributes. When we use machine learning for marketing, clustering can help us identify agreements in groups of prospect customers. Unsupervised learning can help us sort customers into categories that we may not have created using machine learning. It can also help you sort your data when working with a large number of variables.

K-means clustering

K-means clustering works the same way as K-nearest neighbors. You choose a number before k to decide how many groups you want to see. You continue to cluster and repeat until clusters are more clearly classified.

Your data is grouped around centroids, which are the points in your chart that you chose where you want your data clustered. You choose them randomly and you have k. Once you have introduced your data into the model, data points are placed in categories indicated by the nearest center of gravity, which is measured by the Euclidean distance. Then take the average value of the data points around each center of gravity. Keep repeating this process until your results stay the same and you have consistent clusters. Each data point is assigned to only one cluster.

You repeat this process by finding the mean values for x and y within each cluster. This will help you extrapolate the mean value of the data points in each cluster. K-means clustering can help you identify previously unknown or overlooked patterns in the data.

Choose the value for k that is optimal for the number of categories you want to create. Ideally, you should have more than 3. The benefit associated with adding more clusters decreases as the number of clusters increases. The higher the value for k you choose, the smaller and more specific the clusters are. You wouldn't want to use a value for k equal to the number of data points, because each data point would end up in its own cluster.

You should know your dataset well and use your intuition to guess how many clusters are suitable and what kind of differences there will be. However, our intuition and knowledge of the data is less helpful if we have more than just a few potential groups.

Dimensionality reduction

When you use dimension reduction, you shrink data to remove unwanted functions. Simply put, you reduce the number of variables in a data set.

If we have many variables in our model, we run the risk of having dimensionality problems. Dimensionality problems are problems that are unique to models with large data sets and that can affect the accuracy of the prediction. If we have many variables, we need larger populations and sample populations to make our model. With so many variables, it is difficult to have enough data to have many possible combinations to make a well-fitting model.

If we use too many variables, we may also encounter overfitting. Overfitting is the main problem that would make a data scientist think about dimensional reduction.

We must choose data that we do not need or that are not relevant. If we have a model that predicts someone's income, do we need a variable that tells us what their favorite color is? Probably not. We can remove it from our dataset. Usually it is not so easy to determine when to delete a variable. There are some tools we can use to determine which variables are not so important.

Principle Component Analysis is a method to reduce the dimension. We take the old set of variables and somehow convert them into a newer set. The new sets we created are called main components. There is a tradeoff between reducing the number of variables while maintaining the accuracy of your model.

We can also standardize the values of our variables. Make sure that they are all valued on the same relative scale so that you don't blow up the importance of a variable. For example, if we measured variables as a probability between 0 and 1 versus variables measured with whole numbers above 100. Linear discrimination is another method of diminishing the dimension where we combine attributes or variables, rather than removing them altogether.

Kernel Principal Component is the third method of reducing dimensionality. Here variables are placed in a new set. This model will be non-linear and it will give us even better insight into the real parameters than original data.

Neural networks

Neural networks are a form of machine learning called deep learning. It is probably the most advanced machine learning method, and to really understand how it works may require a doctorate. You could write a whole book about machine learning most technical type of model.

Neural networks are computer systems designed to mimic the path of communication in the human brain. In your body you have billions of neurons that are all linked together and travel up through your spine and into your brain. They are connected by root-like nodes that send messages one by one through the neurons all the way up to the chain until it reaches your brain.

While there is no way to replicate this with a computer yet, we take the principle idea and apply it to neural computer networks to replicate the learning ability as a human brain teaches; recognize patterns and derive information from the discovery of new information.

In the case of the neural networks, as with all our machine learning models. Information is processed as numerical data via neural networks. By giving numerical data values, we give it the ability to use algorithms to make predictions.

As with the neurons in the brain, data starts at the top and works down, separating it into nodes first. The neural network uses nodes to communicate through each layer. A neural network consists of three parts; Input, hidden and output layers.

In the image below, we have a visual representation of a neural network, where the circles are each individual node in the network. On the left we have the input layer; this is where our data comes in. After the data has passed through the input layer, it is filtered through several hidden layers. The hidden layers are where data is sorted by different characteristics and functions. The hidden layers search for patterns within the dataset. The hidden layers are where the 'magic' takes place because the data is sorted by patterns that we probably wouldn't recognize if we sort it manually. Each node has a weight that will help determine the meaning of the sorted attribute.

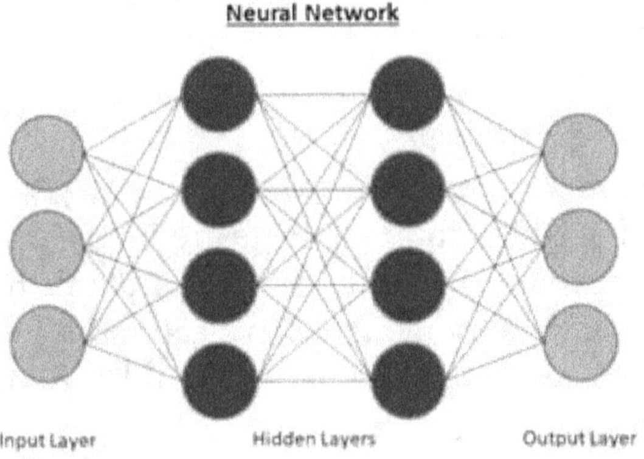

The best use of these neural networks would be a task that would be easy for a human, but extremely difficult for a computer. Think of the beginning of the book when we talked about reasoning and inductive reasoning. Our human brain is a powerful tool for inductive reasoning; it is our advantage over advanced computers that can calculate a large amount of data in seconds. We model neural networks after human thinking because we try to teach a computer how to 'reason' like a human. This is quite a challenge. A good example of a neural network is the example we mentioned, we apply neural networks for tasks that would be very easy for a human, but very challenging for a computer.

Neural networks can take a huge amount of computing power. The first reason neural networks are a challenge to process is because of the amount of data sets needed to create an accurate model. If you want the model to learn how to sort photos, there are many subtle differences between photos that the model must learn to complete the task effectively. This leads to the next challenge, namely the number of variables required for a neural network to function properly. The more data you use and the greater the number of analyzed variables, meaning there is an increase in hidden networks. At any given time, hundreds or even thousands of features are analyzed and classified through the model. Take self-driving cars as an example. Self-driving cars have more than 150 nodes for sorting. This means that the amount of processing power a self-driving car needs to make decisions in a fraction of a second, while analyzing thousands of inputs simultaneously, is quite large.

When sorting photos, neural networks can be very helpful, and the methods used by data scientists are improving quickly. If I showed you a picture of a dog and a picture of a cat, you could easily tell me which was a cat and which was a dog. But a computer requires advanced neural networks and a large amount of data to learn the model.

A common problem with neural networks is overfitting. The model can predict the values for the training data, but when exposed to unknown data it is too specific for the old data and cannot make general predictions for new data.

Suppose a math test is on the way and you want to study. You can remember any formulas that you think will appear on the test and hope that when the test day comes, you can simply connect the new information to what you have already remembered. Or you can study deeper; learn how each formula works so you can get good results even when conditions change. An overfitted model is like memorizing the formulas for a test. It does well if the new data is similar, but if there is a variation it doesn't know how to adjust. You can usually tell if your model is overloaded if it performs well with training data but poorly with test data.

When we check the performance of our model, we can measure it by its cost value. The cost value is the difference between the predicted value and the actual value of our model.

One of the challenges with neural networks is that there is no way to determine the relationship between specific inputs and the output. The hidden layers are called hidden layers for a reason; they are too difficult to interpret or understand.

The most simplistic type of neural network is called a perceptron. It derives its simplicity from the fact that it has only one layer through which data passes. The input layer leads to one classifying hidden layer and the resulting prediction is a binary classification. Remember that when we call a classification technique as binary it means that it only sorts between two different classes, represented by 0 and 1.

The perceptron was first developed by Frank Rosenblatt. It is a good idea to familiarize yourself with the perceptron if you want to learn more about neural networks. The perceptron uses the same process as other neural network models, but you usually work with more layers and more possible outputs. When data is received, the perceptron multiplies the input by the weight it receives. Then the sum of all these values is connected to the activation function. The activation function tells the input what category it falls into, in other words it predicts the output.

If you looked at the perceptron in a graph, the line would look like this:

$f(x) = 0$ if $0 > x$, 1 if $X \geq 0$

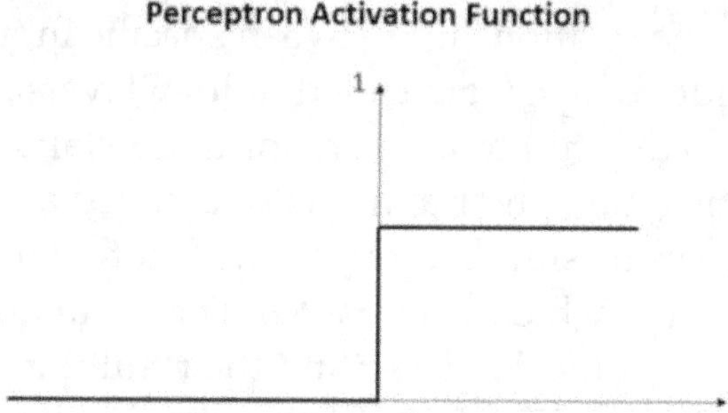

The line of the perception graph appears as a step, with two values, one on each side of the 1. These two sides of the step are the different classes that the model will predict based on the input. As you can see from the graph, it is a bit rough because there is very little separation between the classes. Even a small change in an input variable will cause the predicted output to be a different class. It does not perform as well outside of the original dataset you use for training because it is a step function.

An alternative to the perceptron is a model called a sigmoid neuron. The main advantage of using the sigmoid neuron is that it is not binary. Unlike perceptron, which can classify data into two categories, the sigmoid function creates probability rather than classification. The image below shows the curve of a sigmoid neuron

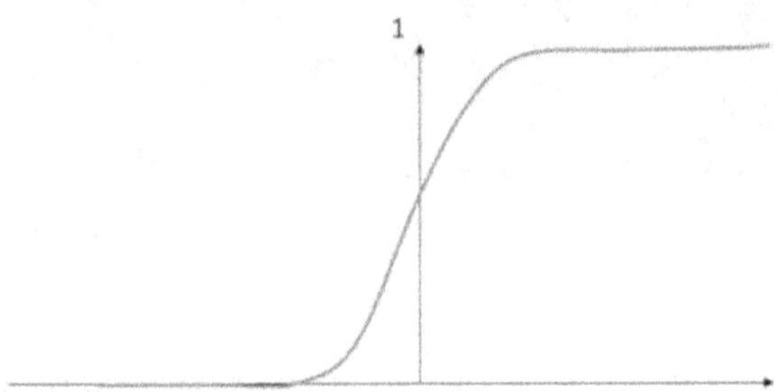

Note the shape of the curve around one, where the data is sorted with the perceptron; the step makes it difficult to classify data with only marginal differences. With the sigmoid neuron, the data is predicted by the probability of falling into a particular class. As you can see, the line curves are at one, which means that the probability of a data point falling into a certain class increases after one, but it's just a probability.

Learning reinforcement

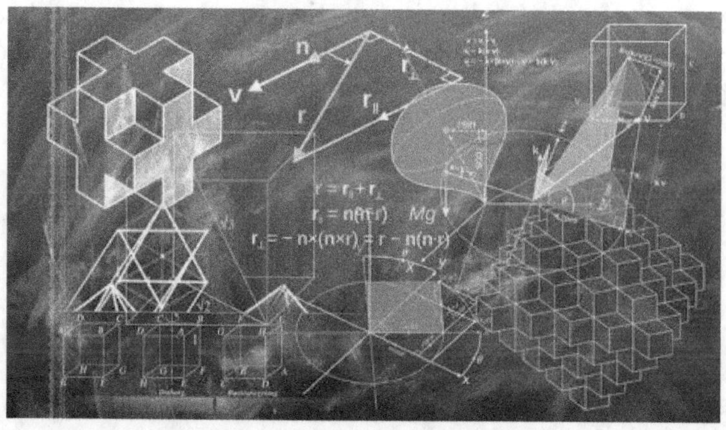

Reinforcement learning is our third type of machine learning. Like unsupervised learning, no input is given. The reinforcement learning model must discover for itself how it can be most effective. Next, the data scientist suggests improving the model based on its ability to predict an outcome, which is evaluated by looking at comparisons between forecast and actual value. This is the most progressive type of machine learning and where much of the machine learning will be done in the future.
Think of it as playing a game; over time you learn by winning and losing. You learn to win by playing and the more you become familiar with the game, the better you understand the mechanics of winning. Over time, the data scientist provides the model with feedback on data collection and processing. It receives a reward signal, so it knows when it predicts an outcome correctly. The game "win" therefore gives positive feedback to the algorithm. This is the type of machine learning used in games, robots, navigation and self-driving cars.

Q Learning

In Q-learning, the model communicates with its environment to improve itself. You start with a series of states. States are the things in the environment that stand as obstacles and roads in your environment. Called "S." In chess, this would be the way all of your pieces can move, as well as where all of your opponent's pieces are located. These are states.

The possible moves are called "A." If you are a pawn, your possible moves are one square forward. If you are a rook, your possible moves are in any direction in a straight line. Q is the value of the model, which starts at 0. As you play the game, Q goes up and down depending on the interactions with the environment. With negative interactions, the score Q decreases. With positive interactions, the score Q increases. The algorithm learns how to move so it can optimize the number Q. It is random at first. Over time, these random movements result in positive and negative effects on Q, and the machine learns how each movement will affect the score of Q. It has to play a lot of games to improve the way it plays over time. It is much easier said than done to apply this process in real life.

SARSA State Action Reward State Action There is only a slight difference between SARSA and Q. They work the same way to give the model a reward response.

Deep Q network Deep Q is used when ordinary Q is not general enough. When he sees new things he has never seen before, he doesn't know what to do. Q learning cannot adapt itself for things he has never seen. Deep Q uses a neural network.

Markov Decision Process has a set of possible states, a set of models, a set of possible actions and a real value reward. This model learns through interaction with the environment through continuous interaction.

DDPG Deeply deterministic policy development Another reward state model functions as an actor and critic.

Semi-guided learning

This type of machine learning uses a combination of guided and unaccompanied learning. Some data is labeled, while others are not. But most of the time, most of the data is not labeled. Semi-guided learning can be used for classification, regression and prediction.

Semi-supervised machine learning is useful because labeling everything is too time consuming and can damage the ability to find new patterns.

Ensemble Modelling

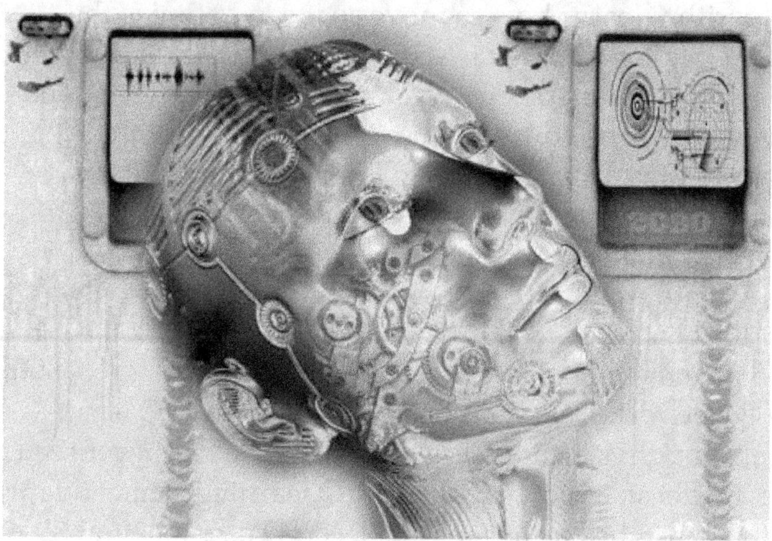

We have learned that diversifying our trees can create a more accurate prediction. But what if, instead of using different versions of the same model, we just used different models? This is a common trick in machine learning, also known as ensemble modeling. By combining information from multiple different types of algorithms, we can improve the accuracy and predictability of our model.

Ensemble modeling is all about the division and victory mentality. Different models give us different insights about the data that may not be recognizable for other models. By combining the information from different models, we can learn even more about the truth of our data.

Ensemble modeling also helps minimize bias and variance in our predictions. Individual models may contain prediction errors, but the sum of all our predictions will be more accurate.

There are a few different methods of using ensemble modeling:

The first is to take the mode of your predictions. That is, take the value most common with the models. Whichever prediction occurs most often or has the highest number of "votes" is the prediction we choose.

We can also take the average of all predictions depending on the type of models we have. The average of all predictions becomes our final prediction. Our ensemble must also take into account the reliability of individual models. The results of our models are given different weights, making some predictions more important than others based on reliability.

How do we know what kind of models we want to combine? We already know from this book that there are different types of models to choose from, each with different capabilities and benefits.

A common pair of models use neural networks and decision trees together. Neural networks provide us with new information and the decision tree ensures that we have not missed anything.

In addition to the bootstrapping and bagging we discussed earlier, there are a few other ways to do ensemble modeling. Data scientists use a so-called bucket of models. Here they use different types of models to use with the test data and then choose the one that performed best.

Another idea is called stacking. Stacking uses different types of models and then uses all the results to give us a prediction that is a combination of all.

Data scientists like to use ensemble modeling because we can usually make better predictions with a variety of models than with a single model alone.

The downside of ensemble modeling is that we lose some of our legibility. Having multiple models at the same time makes interpretation more difficult, especially if you want to share the data with stakeholders who have no knowledge of data science.

We can also use different versions of the same model, such as how random forests improve prediction with multiple versions of themselves - using neural networks with different sets of nodes and different values for k, or numbers of clusters to see how that changes the outcome of our prediction and find out if there is an optimal value for k, or if there are any groups or subgroups that we may have overlooked.

It doesn't do much if we already have a strong model. But if we combine a few models with weaker forecast capabilities, it usually improves overall accuracy.

Things you need to know for machine learning

To be successful with machine learning, you need to have the right tools to work, just as you should have skills and the necessary tools when building a house. Below is a list of the materials needed to do machine learning.

Data

In order to work with your data, you must have enough data to divide it into two categories; training data and test data. Training data is the data that you initially use when building your model. When you first create your model, you need to give it some data to learn from. With training data you already know the independent variables and their respective dependent variables. This means that for every input you already know the output of your data. Based on this data, your model learns to predict the output itself. Our training data gives us the parameters we need to make predictions. This is the data our machine learns from.
Test data is the data the machine receives as soon as you are satisfied with the model and see what it does in the wild. In this data, we only have the independent variables, but no output. With test data, we can see how well our model predicts a result with new data.

Your training data should contain most of your data; about 70%, while your test data is the remaining 30%. To avoid bias, make sure that the data you choose for training data and test data is completely random when you split them. Do not choose which data you want to use; let it be random. Do not use the same data for training and testing. Start by giving the training data to the machine and investigate the relationships between X and Y, then try to see how well your model performed.

The main question to consider during this process is whether your model will still work when presented with new data. You can test this through cross validation. This means that you will test your model for data that you have not yet used. Have some data on hand that you have not used during training to see how accurate your model is at the end.

You can also use K-fold validation to check the accuracy of your model. This method is quite easy to use and generally unbiased. It's a good technique to use if we don't have a lot of data to test with. For K-fold validation, we will split our data into K-folds, usually between 5 and 10. Test each fold and see how they performed over all folds when you are done testing. Usually, the larger your number for k, the less biased your test will be.

So far we've talked about models that interpret data to find meaning and patterns. But what kind of data are we going to use? Where do we get our data from and what does it look like?

Data is the most critical part of machine learning. After all, your model only learns with data, so it is important that you have relevant and meaningful data. It came in many shapes and sizes, different structure depending on the types of data. The more structured the data, the easier it is to work with. Some data have a very small structure and these data are more difficult to interpret. Face recognition data can be huge and has little meaning to the untrained eye.

Structured data is better organized. This is the type of data you are likely to use when you first start. It will help get your feet wet and you can start understanding the statistic involved in machine learning. Structure data usually comes in a familiar form that looks something like this, in rows and columns. This is called a table dataset.

Market Value	num_bedrooms	num_bathrooms	Sq_ft	pool (Y/N)
$207,367	4	3	2635	N
$148,224	3	2	1800	Y
$226,897	5	3.5	2844	Y
$122,265	2	1.5	1644	N

The main question to consider during this process is whether your model will still work when presented with new data. You can test this through cross validation. This means that you will test your model for data that you have not yet used. Have some data on hand that you have not used during training to see how accurate your model is at the end.

You can also use K-fold validation to check the accuracy of your model. This method is quite easy to use and generally unbiased. It's a good technique to use if we don't have a lot of data to test with. For K-fold validation, we will split our data into K-folds, usually between 5 and 10. Test each fold and see how they performed over all folds when you are done testing. Usually, the larger your number for k, the less biased your test will be.

So far we've talked about models that interpret data to find meaning and patterns. But what kind of data are we going to use? Where do we get our data from and what does it look like?

Data is the most critical part of machine learning. After all, your model only learns with data, so it is important that you have relevant and meaningful data. It came in many shapes and sizes, different structure depending on the types of data. The more structured the data, the easier it is to work with. Some data have a very small structure and these data are more difficult to interpret. Face recognition data can be huge and has little meaning to the untrained eye.

Structured data is better organized. This is the type of data you are likely to use when you first start. It will help get your feet wet and you can start understanding the statistic involved in machine learning. Structure data usually comes in a familiar form that looks something like this, in rows and columns. This is called a table dataset.

Prepare the data

So now you have your data, but how do you get it to a point where it is readable by your model? Data seldom fits directly with our modeling needs. In order to properly format our data, a round of data cleanup is usually required first. The data cleaning process is often referred to as data scrubbing. We may have data in the form of images or emails. We have to rewrite it so that it has numerical values that can be interpreted by our algorithms. After all, our machine learning models are algorithms or mathematical equations, so the data must have numerical values to be modeled.

You may also have pieces of data that are recorded incorrectly or in the wrong format. There may be variables you don't need and need to get rid of. It can be tedious and time consuming, but it is extremely important to have data that works and can be easily read by your model. It is the least sexy part of a data scientist.

This is the part of machine learning where you are likely to spend the most time. As a data scientist, you probably spend about 20% of your time on data science and the other 80% of your time making sure your data is clean and ready to be processed by your model. We may combine multiple types of data and we will need to reformat the recordings to match them. First, in the case of guided learning, choose the variables that you think are most important to your model. Choosing irrelevant variables or variables that don't matter can cause bias and make our model less effective.

A simple example of cleaning or scrubbing data is recoding a response for gender. On your data you have a column for male / female. Unfortunately, men and women have no numerical value. But you can easily change this by making it a binary variable. Assign female = 1 and male = 0. Now you can find a numerical value for the effect that being a woman has on the outcome of your model.

We can also combine variables to make it easier to interpret. Let's say you create a regression model that predicts a person's income based on several variables. One of the variables is the level of education, which you have recorded in years. So the possible responses for years of education are 1, 2, 3, 4, 5, 6, 7, 8, 9, 10, 11, 12, 13, 14, 15, 16. These are many separate categories. You could simplify it by creating groups. For example, you can rewrite variables 1, 2, 3, 4, 5, 6, 7, 8 = primary_ed and rewrite 9, 10, 11, 12 = secondary_ed and rewrite 13, 14, 15, 16 = tertiary education. Instead of twelve categories, you have three. Respondents have either a basic education, secondary education, or a level of post-secondary or university education. This is known as binning data and it can be a good way to clean up your data if used properly.

When you combine variables to make interpretation easier, you have to balance more streamlined data with losing important information about relationships in the data. Note that in this example, by combining these variables into three groups instead of sixteen, you create bias in your model. There are many factors that can cause you to clean your data. Even a misspelling or an extra space somewhere in your data can have a negative effect on your model.

You may have missing data. To fix this situation, you can replace the missing values with the mode of the median of that variable. It is possible to delete data with missing values if there are only a few, but this just means you have to use less data in your model.

Programming tools

To process your data, you need special programming tools so you can tell the data what you want them to do. We have already mentioned that machine learning is a branch of computer science. This is where that comes into play.

In the introduction, we said that the three most common languages for data science are Python, R and C ++. Choosing the right one depends on your experience and what you plan to do with your data.

The most common language for data science is python. It was created in 1991 by Guido Van Rossum and it is notable for being easier to read than other programming languages. It is still being developed and improved. It is not complicated to learn and is compatible
with the most relevant data types. It also has applications beyond data manipulation that will be useful in machine learning.

Python has several free packages that you can install that were created to give you shortcuts to commonly used data science tools. These packages contain shortcuts to codes often used in machine learning, so you have less work to do.

Pandas is an indispensable library of tools for data scientists working with python. This makes it easier to manipulate time series data and table data series. It shows your data in rows and columns so that it is easier to manage, the same way you would look at data in Microsoft Excel. It is easy to find online and free to download. Pandas are useful when looking at datasets in .CSV format.

Numpy is a useful program to process data faster with python. It works in the same way as Matlab and it can process matrices and multidimensional data. It will help you import large data sets more easily.

Scikit-learn is another library of the machine learning function. With Scikit learn, you have easy access to many of the algorithms we mentioned earlier, which are often used in machine learning. Algorithms like classification, regression, clustering, support vector, arbitrary forest and k resources have shortcuts so much of the grunt coding is done for you.

R is the third option. It is free to use and open source. R can be used for both data mining and machine learning. It is popular for those new to data science because of its availability. It can't handle the larger datasets required for more advanced machine learning operations, but it's not a bad place to start if you're new to data science and computer programming.

You need a computer to run these programs. Usually a regular laptop or desktop computer is powerful enough to handle smaller and medium data sets, especially if you are new to machine learning.

While Graphics Processing Units (GPUs) have been around for some time, their accessibility has increased in recent years, making data science more accessible. It is a breakthrough in data science because the field is no longer limited to labs with huge computers.

GPUs are known as the power behind video games. This allows a computer to interpret multiple points at once, which is essential for processing large amounts of data. With GPUs, we can now do much more with much less computer hardware. The predecessor, CPU cores, control multiple control units, allowing information to be processed in one go. Rather than having multiple control units, the GPU has a much larger web of cores that can all handle different processes at once. One GPU card can contain nearly 5000 processors. It is a major advance for artificial intelligence and machine learning. They can help speed up the processing of neural networks.

C and C ++ are other commonly used languages for data analysis. The advantage of C ++ is that it is a very powerful language. It can process huge data sets very quickly. Data scientists who use massive data sets often choose to use C ++ because of its speed and processing power, especially when working with data sets over a terabyte. C ++ can process one gigabyte of data in about a second. This makes it especially useful for deep learning algorithms, 5-10 layer neural network models and huge data sets. This type of model can be overwhelming for software that is not so fast. If you are doing more advanced machine learning and you have multiple GPUs, then C ++ may be the language for you. C ++ can do almost anything; it is a very versatile language.

The downside is that the libraries in C ++ are not as extensive as those in Python. This means that when you write code for your data and model, you probably start from scratch. No matter what kind of projects you decide to do, there will be roadblocks as you write your code. Having a library that can help you when you get stuck helps you learn and work faster.

Develop models

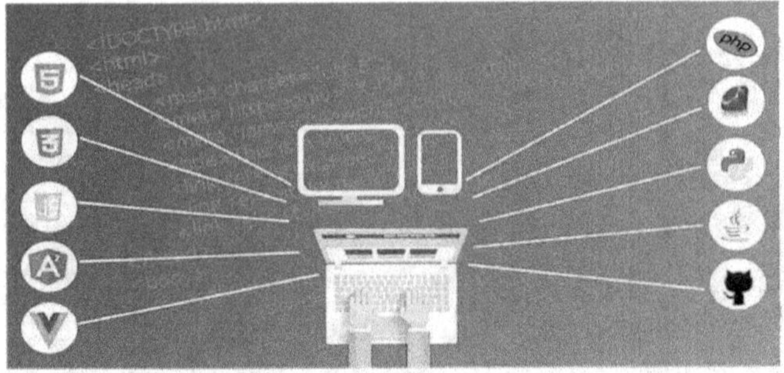

You must set up in Python or another programming language to learn machine learning. You create machine learning models by using code to manipulate the datasets. While this book does not cover machine learning coding, I will give you a brief overview of some basic libraries and packages that I recommend you install for machine learning.

Since this is the most widely used language in data science, we will use Python as an example in this chapter. I also think it is the most practical language to learn if it is your first language because it is more readable than other programming languages, and it has a wide range of possibilities beyond machine learning.

Once you have the latest version of Python installed, there are a few recommended libraries to install that contain many commands that can be useful for your machine learning work. All of these can be easy to find with a quick Google search and they can be downloaded for free.

The main library for data analysis and machine learning in Python is called Pandas. It's a fairly popular choice for data sets and will make your encoding easier and faster, especially if you're still trying to get a feel for things.

Anaconda for python

Another option to get started with Python is to install Anaconda. The great thing about Anaconda is that it gives you every package for Python, so you don't have to install the packages one by one while writing the program for your model. It comes with all the libraries you need, for just about every other kind of function.

Anaconda is a free and open source program that works in both R and Python. With Anaconda you have access to various libraries that will help you with your data science projects. This basically gives you a prepackaged collection of all python libraries, of which there are over 100 libraries.

One of the main libraries is Spyder and Jupyter. Both are integrated development environments, meaning they are the window where you will write your code, but they are more developed than a standard command window and have options to store and export / import codes.

Most Python users start in a development environment called IDLE. It is very simple and offers a good format for learning to code in python. When you install Python on a Windows computer, it is included automatically. If you have a Linux computer, it is available, but you must install it separately. IDLE makes those little steps in Python easier because you can save your scripts and edit them later. It will also help you debug.

To install Anaconda, go to:

docs.anaconda.com/anaconda/install

Scroll down until you see a list of operating systems. Choose your operating system. It gives you instructions on how to install anaconda on their website based on your operating system. Then you are ready to mess around in Python. I highly recommend using one of the free Python beginner tutorials available on the web. EdX has a free beginner's guide in Python, which is a great place to start. Also take advantage of forums such as Reddit, where a large number of frequently asked questions have already been answered in detail and members always share relevant news from the world of machine learning.

Algorithms

Once you have your data and the hardware and software to manipulate it, you need to bring them together. Put your data on your programming software. Find a free dataset online to work with when you first start. Kaggle.com is free and has many datasets to choose from in CSV format, which you can easily work with once you have imported the Pandas library into your Python.

The best algorithms to start with are linear and logistic regression for guided learning and clusters of k-means in unsupervised learning. These will start relatively easily and you can build to other models from there.

Visualization tools

You have your data, and now you have made models using one of the programming languages, and you have a whole collection of data science libraries to help you do all this faster. Your computer works well and you can make models independently.

You may have created models that yield interesting results, but to break it down into lay terms and communicate your findings to stakeholders, you need to organize it in a way that is easy to visualize. If you're a data scientist in a marketing project, you may have created a model that allows you to categorize customers and predict trends in buying habits. But if you want to communicate these results to the rest of your marketing team, you need to find a way to communicate so that even people who not familiar with data science can understand your results. By splitting your data into graphs and charts and visually, you can supplement your analytical skills. Being able to create visualizations of your data is extremely important when communicating with an audience unfamiliar with data analysis

A popular toolset for data professionals is Tableau. Such tools are called data visualization software. Some companies have employees whose entire job is to take hard-to-read data and present it in a way that is easy to visualize.

Software such as tableau is very often used by companies that rely on data to make decisions. Tableau is useful because it is relatively easy to use and data can be viewed through the platform in real time. You can customize a dashboard of tools for creating reports and charts with your data. It also gives you the opportunity to share your results with other people in your company. Tableau can be used to create graphs and scatter plots of that data that you have analyzed in your programming language.

More advanced things that are useful

These tools may not be as relevant to you when you are just starting out, but it can be interesting to talk about some of them and think about what might be useful later. This book may just be the beginning of your path to becoming a machine learning expert, so you can refer to this list later if you're a little more advanced.

You need to keep thinking about managing unstructured data. Usually this requires more advanced programs because it is more difficult to manage and manipulate. This type of data often takes the form of something way too complicated for the human brain to analyze without the help of tools, but this is the direction machine learning is heading. Using neural networks to mimic the functions of human thinking, who knows what the future holds.

The further we get with machine learning, the bigger our data becomes. The possibilities of machine learning are increasing. The data that will be important in the future does not have the neat structure that we are used to, like the kind of data that fits in an Excel sheet.

This type of data also requires more powerful computer hardware and software to handle the processing of these large amounts of information. Usually use some kind of cloud computing software to transport the large amounts of information, as well as a GPU specific for data analysis. This higher calculation level can help to process multiple moving points at the same time. The required math is also getting more difficult. Combine algorithms.

Epilogue

Hopefully, after reading this book, you will have a good understanding of the basics of machine learning. You have now become acquainted with various types of popular machine learning models and their uses. We explored how advanced data scientists use machine learning to make predictions and the parameters they need to make predictions that are accurate and reliable when introduced into new data. The great thing about data science and machine learning is the wide range of applications. If you go out and gain experience with machine learning, there is a wide range of jobs and opportunities that work with all kinds of data. Whether you like the competition and crowds, and you want to use models that predict the rise and fall of stocks or guess what a customer will buy next. Or maybe you are interested in medicine and healthcare; you can apply machine learning to improve cancer diagnosis and gain new insight into the characteristics of a disease and how it will affect different individuals. Wherever your interests lie, there is a chance that machine learning will be implanted to improve what we can already do.

The more the world becomes connected, the more data becomes available. Almost everyone has some kind of smart device registration and tracking their user data. Data scientists find more creative ways to learn from and interpret that data. Machine learning is a way for data scientists to explore trends beyond the scope of human understanding, meaning that our predictions will remain more accurate and our data will be more useful.

Computers will only get more powerful and that power will become more and more accessible, which means that machine learning and data science are no longer just buzzwords, but commonly used methods to find valuable information. It is not only large companies that make more use of data and machine learning; It is becoming easier for even smaller companies to include big data in their decision-making processes.

Now that you know the basic theory of machine learning, it's time to move on and find ways to apply and practice the knowledge. If you're interested in being a data scientist specializing in machine learning, this book is just the beginning of the process. I strongly recommend that you commit yourself to learn a language like Python, R or C ++. The next step is to become a data scientist and apply these theories of machine learning in actual models and algorithms. Thanks to the Internet, there are a large number of free books, videos and tutorials available that will guide you through the process of learning computer languages. There has never been a better time to learn how to code and make your own models. This book is only a small part of a large collection of information available on the subject. If you take machine learning seriously, this isn't the only book you read.

You can find whole books that describe the process of specific models. Neural networks are an area so advanced that you could find entire books based on that specific type of model alone. It's not a bad idea to pick up a few statistical study guides so you can refer to them if you have a question. Be on the lookout for potential data sources you could potentially use and potential questions that might be interesting to research with statistical math.

The vacancies alone are sufficient reason to pursue further knowledge in the field. There is a shortage of experienced data scientists who can apply the methods and techniques mentioned in this book. This means there is an opportunity for someone who wants to get their hands dirty and start coding their own models. There are companies and organizations that are currently looking for people who can make good use of this information. Keep in mind that this question will not exist forever. Universities all over the world are already creating new courses that specifically focus on data science as a mix of computer science and statistics. This means that the next generation of data scientists is already on the way.

So start learning now. Find an online tutorial and some free datasets online and find out how to use regression and classifications, using this book as a guide. Learn each model one by one. Search the web for examples of completed models and see if you can replicate the results. Learning programming languages takes time, so be patient and find new opportunities to learn and adjust your skills.

Try one of the online communities specific to statistical modeling to cut your teeth and learn from what other data scientists do. I recommend you check out Kaggle.com. It is a website that organizes statistical modeling competitions for aspiring data scientists. Various companies and organizations place competitions with the supplied datasets. It's a great way to experiment with different tasks and get data to work. Old contests are also available online, with a host of accompanying tutorials on youtube.com and other data science communities for you to learn from. It is probably the best way for an aspiring data scientist to expand his / her resume and network with other data scientists.